GOOD DOG!

Educating the family pet

GOOD DOG!

Educating the family pet

Ann Head

Illustrations directed by Ann Head
photographed by Arthur Sidey (Daily Mirror)

Popular Dogs
London Sydney Auckland Johannesburg

Popular Dogs Publishing Co. Ltd

An imprint of Century Hutchinson Ltd
Brookmount House, 62–65 Chandos Place,
Covent Garden, London WC2N 4NW
Century Hutchinson Australia (Pty) Ltd
20 Alfred Street, Milsons Point, Sydney 2061
Century Hutchinson New Zealand Limited
191 Archers Road, PO Box 40–086, Glenfield, Auckland 10
Century Hutchinson South Africa (Pty) Ltd
PO Box 337, Bergvlei 2012, South Africa

First published 1987
Reprinted in paperback 1988, 1989
Copyright © Ann Head 1987

Set in Sabon

Printed by Butler & Tanner Ltd,
Frome and London

British Library Cataloguing in Publication Data
Head, Ann.
Good dog!: educating the family pet.
1. Pets: Dogs. Training—Manuals
I. Title
636.7′083

ISBN 0 09 174037 1

Frontispiece: *Two of our young students. Holly* (left) *and Duffy –
litter sister and brother age* $3\frac{1}{2}$ *months when the photo was taken*

**To the dog
for the pleasure of his company!**

About the Author

Ann Head worked for six and a half years in Los Angeles where she was personal assistant trainer to Frank Inn, the now retired coach behind the multi-million dollar movie star dog, Benji. During that period, Ann became a member of the Union for Professional Motion Picture Animal Trainers in Hollywood, working on Benji features, TV specials and countless other productions featuring Frank Inn animals.

Now back home in England, Ann Head has established a stable of stars including Arthur the paw-dipping cat, Danny the talking Jack Russell, Oliver the ginger tom famous for his spectacular leaps across the TV screen in the cat food commercials, Sophie the feline virtuoso of the piano and, of course, Pippin the greatest ham of them all. Granddaughter of Benji, Pippin cut her teeth on the major sound stages around Hollywood. Now the star of the TV series 'Woof' as well as of the RSPCA public information film 'Too Late for Tessie', numerous commercials and community films shown in schools by 43 police forces, she is also a truly international model and her pictures are syndicated around the globe.

Arthur Sidey has been a *Daily Mirror* staff photographer for forty years. His animal photography is famous the world over and his pictures feature in many national newspapers.

Publisher's Note

The veterinary content of this book has been checked and endorsed by Tim Davies BVSC, MRCVS, of the Nine Mile Veterinary Hospital, Wokingham, Berkshire

Contents

Our third student, Bruno, at five months (litter brother to Holly and Duffy)

Introduction

One may take a riding crop and, with just a fair correction, encourage a horse to perform to order; or one may flog it unmercifully! The decision lies with us and our consciences.

Pets or working animals have no means of answering back. We keep them in a domestic environment, beholden to us for food, health and shelter. We restrict most of them in such a way that they cannot escape our premises, either because we need to make use of their working abilities or for our amusement and pleasure. If we treat them badly, only God can help them.

Dog ownership means a great deal more than just putting a bowl of food down once a day.

Think about it!

I

A good dog for you

Dog ownership should be a lifetime commitment, ideally until your pal dies of old age or your vet decides that in his opinion it would be a kindness to end the dog's days in this world, to avoid unnecessary suffering.

Puppies should never be impulse buys. They require full-time responsibility and care and a great deal of thought should be put into the breed and type chosen. Consider every aspect of your lifestyle before you make a move, and even when you have decided upon a particular 'make' don't just rush to the yellow pages and dash down to the nearest breeder who may have 'just one left', the one she had 'intended keeping for herself'. Look at it by all means, it may be ideal, but *do* take your time and shop around. Go, if possible, to a few shows where your chosen breed is being exhibited. Championship shows are the best as the exhibits are usually the cream of the crop and the dogs are 'benched', which means that they are secured in stalls arranged in long rows and numbered in sequence, making it easy to ascertain just who is who. Many good dogs are exhibited at 'open' shows, but by and large the standard is not quite so high and as there is seldom any benching it may often be difficult to find the person or dog you are looking for. These open shows are often held in local parks. Either type of show will be advertised in the popular dog publications so buy one and look for the forthcoming dates in your area.

If you decide to visit a championship show, walk around the benches with a catalogue and check off the numbers with the names of the breeders, then approach their dogs with caution and test for temperament first. Dogs that 'fly out' from the benches are nasty and nervous. Don't be fobbed off by the owners who will say that they are behaving normally because they are 'on guard'. They should *not* fly out at all and sundry in a public place where they may be approached by an innocent child who could get bitten in the face. It is unnecessary for show dogs to behave in this way and I will not accept any excuse for it. Dogs may guard their premises at home.

This is fine, providing the situation is under control, but not in public! If they have been trained to behave in this manner, their owners are *very* irresponsible. *No* – if you are told any 'tales' regarding the reasons for the dog being aggressive, treat them with a pinch of salt. Ideally, just go up to the sweet, gentle, professional animals who usually have owners to match, and ask their folks if you may visit their kennels. If they have a waiting list for puppies this usually means that the little dog will be worth having, even if there is a bit of a delay.

If you can spare the time it is fun to go and see the dogs in their home environment and very enlightening. One can usually assess the situation in a very short time when one sees how the animals are kept and treated. *Always* ask to meet the mother of the puppies and Dad too if he is around. If not, ask who he is and check through the breed registrations or get the address from the owners of the dam, and if the sire is not too far away, pop in and visit him also. Responsible professional breeders welcome visitors and are usually proud to show off dogs that pass on good type and temperament.

Temperament is *everything*! Nervous dogs are frequently 'fear biters', who will back away from humans and will try to protect themselves by snapping if approached. This is a terribly sad situation and often results in the animal being put down and I have to say (dog lover though I am) that in many cases it is the only kind solution. A dog *born* nervous cannot ever really be *completely* cured. It will always retain its in-built fears, although these fears can be kept under control by people who really understand the situation, and the nervousness can be very well disguised in the show ring by clever handlers. However, the fact remains that a dog with an inborn nervous disposition can never be totally predictable. It will often be doted on by its owners and, of course, in its home environment will behave impeccably. It is only when faced with the unexpected that a nasty situation could materialize. The sad fact is that many novice owners of such dogs see no fault in them and will often try to reassure their pet when it starts to bark or behave aggressively in public. This can do nothing but inflame the situation as the dog has no idea that he is doing wrong. His owners love him and they see no reason to offer any correction. No! Steer clear of a nervous puppy unless you are highly experienced and you have a specific reason (although I can't for the life of me think of one) for taking it. Novice owners of nervous dogs are like the blind leading the blind . . . anything can happen.

Now a timid 'thinker' is another story. My own Pippin was one of these. She is the type who as a youngster would seek a safe place to cross the river whilst her happy-go-lucky dumb brother would jump in with gay abandon and nearly drown. What I am trying to say is that there is the dog who is so darned smart that he will assess every situation before making a move (and why not?). Very sensible, but this can easily be mistaken for a backer-off or fear-biter.

It really takes an expert to distinguish between the two when a puppy is very young. Pippin was extremely timid as a baby and would jump at her own shadow, but with gentle handling she has become a star. This situation can be achieved if the dog is taught every new behaviour sympathetically, step by step, building confidence until the end result is an outgoing, happy animal. Bear in mind, however, that Pippin has *never* shown aggressive behaviour towards humans – only timidity, which can be overcome in time.

This method of development also works well with a dog that has become **environmentally** nervous through no fault of his own: the dog who has suffered at the hands of man and lost his confidence. This can be restored in time in an animal who was born with a strong disposition but has had his confidence shattered by ill treatment. These cases are so rewarding but need the patience of Job himself. What an achievement though, when one restores the love and trust in humans that looked as if it had been lost forever!

So much for the nervous puppy. So which one should you buy? I personally recommend the nice 'middle of the road' little fellow. *Not* the one who sits at the back and won't approach strangers, and not the bubbly one who dashes out to the front. The latter may well be (and probably is) fine, but the sensible one who will sit and look at you and weigh up the situation first, demonstrates that he has a few brains. The little thinker will probably approach in time, and once he has decided that all is well he will be beside himself with doggie greetings. *This is a good dog!* Once he has convinced himself that everything is o.k. he will be your friend for life. But the fact that he thought about it for a moment means that he is probably a cut above the rest for brains and good material for training. A fine happy-go-lucky puppy is great, of course, but remember that there are *two* types of nervous dog and some are so lively that they can border on being hyper-active. These are the excitable 'pee-ers', the ones who piddle as they wag their tails. Not very desirable really, especially on your best friend's carpet. Yes, they are friendly all right, but how friendly do you need? Try to go for the nice common-sense, no-nonsense dog who is gentle and affectionate, outgoing without being hyper. It's asking for the moon, but they are around. If in doubt ask for advice. Many vets are only too happy to help a prospective client. They will certainly assess horses for would-be owners and some will help with the selection of a good puppy. If not, try to find someone with a lot of experience in dogs and pick their brains.

It should be taken as 'read' that all this goes for non-pedigree dogs as well. Mongrels are super, absolutely super. I love them. They are certainly tougher in many ways than their pedigree cousins. They won't cost you so much at the vet's, that's for sure. They have hardly any hereditary defects as they are so outcrossed. Consequently, you can usually expect your mongrel to enjoy a long and healthy life.

Each time a baby mongrel comes into the world God breaks the mould, so if you like the idea of owning an 'exclusive edition' then this is the dog for you. No two mongrels are exactly alike. One may well argue that no two pedigree dogs are *exactly* alike and their breeders will always be able to tell the difference, but the fact remains that a row of beautiful Golden Cocker Spaniels from the same litter look like peas in a pod, but a row of mongrel litter mates will probably be liquorice allsorts. (See photograph of Pippin with her trunk full of 'dolly mixtures' on page 117.) I love all dogs, with or without aristocratic backgrounds, but I have to say that I do have a special place in my heart for the mongrel. They are mostly smart little critters and very rarely nervous. Structurally they are, of course, a bit of a gamble as one never quite knows for certain how they will turn out looks-wise. What may appear to be smooth-coated at eight weeks may grow into a shaggy 'door mat' dog by twelve months. However, if you are prepared for any eventuality regarding your dog's appearance and will just accept him for himself, he will give you a lifetime of trust and devotion.-

Big feet often indicate a large dog to come, but not always! It *is* a gamble, but as a rule of thumb, if a mongrel puppy is around five to eight inches tall at eight weeks, he should usually stay well below knee height at maturity.

However, there are always exceptions to every rule. *Please* be prepared for any development in height and looks before taking on a baby mongrel. He will change and it won't be his fault if he ends up with one ear up and the other down. He will love you for yourself, warts and all, and hopefully you will offer the same in return. If you have the slightest doubt and you feel that you would prefer a 'tailor-made' model, go for a pedigree. It is downright cruelty to keep a little dog for a few months only to shatter his confidence by getting rid of him because you don't like the way he has turned out. Totally irresponsible in fact!

Of course, one can always rescue a 'ready made' one from the animal shelter. At least this way if you choose a young adult mongrel you know exactly what you are getting from the point of view of size and type. Again, temperament is very important. One must ask oneself the question, 'Why is he here?' Sometimes the kennel girls know the history and it is always worth asking. Maybe he wasn't a stray at all, but brought in because of the family moving abroad or the arrival of a new baby (very common, this, and worth thinking about yourself if you are newly married). Ask if you can take the dog out of the pen and walk him up and down on the lead. See if he seems gentle and friendly. Most rescue dogs seem *so* grateful that they almost know that they must remain on their best behaviour. They are very rewarding and well worth considering. If you save a dog from the animal shelter do consider having him completely groomed out (see chapter 8, page 82) before taking him into your home, no matter now clean and healthy he may appear. Just as a precaution.

One final point. The last place one should go to buy a puppy is to a dealer. One can never be sure of the health and background. You may be lucky, but it is far too great a gamble when you can go directly to a breeder and see the litter and parents 'first hand'. There is also the matter of pedigree papers. If you are a first-time buyer of a purebred dog, remember that the pedigree is not worth the paper it is written on unless it is accompanied by the Kennel Club *transfer of ownership form*. This must be *signed by the breeder* and given to you on the day you buy your puppy.

The actual pedigree is just that, and no more: a mere record of the puppy's ancestry and if you have no intention of either breeding or showing your dog it is just a nice thing to have so you can look back with interest at all his illustrious forebears. Unless the actual ownership of the dog is transferred to you, technically the puppy is *still the property of the breeder.* The transfer paper is absolutely essential if you wish to breed or show in the future.

Some breeders don't bother to register puppies with minor faults and sell them as 'pet quality only'. This is fine, as long as they make the situation absolutely clear to you at the time you buy. Then you will probably just get the pedigree alone, on the written understanding that the puppy is to be a family pet and not intended for either breeding or showing. You may be asked to sign some form of agreement stating that you clearly understand this at the time of purchase. Usually these puppies are very good value as they are considerably cheaper than their top-class brothers and sisters, and so long as they are happy and healthy you may well get a bargain!

2

Home and dry

On the day you go to collect your new puppy, ask for a diet sheet or just take a note of what he has been fed and the amounts etc., to avoid an upset tum. With the change of environment your little friend will have plenty to cope with, and a strange food may well be the last straw and give him the 'runs'. Not very desirable when you are hoping to house-train him as soon as possible. Make certain that he is fully relieved before he leaves his old home premises. Do *not* stop on the way back under any circumstances to give him a break and a 'quick one' on the grass verge. Why? Because if he has no vaccinations to protect him he must not come into contact with the outside world until two weeks after his second injection, which will probably be at about twelve to fourteen weeks, depending upon your vet. Some vets vaccinate at eight to ten weeks and some later, often according to the size and maturity of your puppy.

You may ferry him home in one of several ways, but I find a small carry box is very good if it contains some old clean towels, covered with several layers of kitchen roll. This method is ideal if you have a long journey because in the event of his vomiting or just relieving himself through excitement, he will at least be contained and your car will remain clean. Place the box on the back seat and have someone sit next to it to constantly reassure and chat to him. If he vomits it is far better that it happens in the car than to run the risk of setting him down outside. I usually take loads of extra kitchen roll with me when I collect a new animal, just in case. If you can keep his attention, all will be well and he won't worry himself into a sickly situation. Eventually on a long run he will probably doze off. (For more information on travel sickness, see 'Diet and Health Care', page 72.)

Home at last! The children (if any) are thrilled! What fun! What excitement! What total bewilderment for a little chap who has just left his Mum behind. *Do* try to contain your understandable enthusiasm. Try hard (I know it's not easy) to keep everything very low key on his first day. Immediately he is out of the car, *carried* of course (especially if your driveway is open plan!), let him potter in the back garden in a spot where you feel it will be o.k. for him to establish a toilet area. (Say, by the compost heap!) Stay with him and try to encourage him to remain in the vicinity until he eventually lets rip, hopefully doing two jobs. Then, and only then, let him indoors.

If you really want to own the ultimate dog with regard to toilet training and you would like him always to use the same spot in the garden, this can very easily be achieved by surrounding the spot with some low chicken wire and each time you let your puppy out to 'take a break' carry him to the area and pop him over the netting, staying with him for reassurance. He *must* go eventually and he has no alternative but to do it there. If this routine is followed religiously by **every member of the family**, the little dog will soon *associate* toilets with that area alone and it makes cleaning up much easier. No-one really likes to see piles of 'poop' in the middle of the lawn and it can be avoided very easily. It is just a matter of common sense.

Eventually your new arrival will be able to trot down the garden behind you to his designated spot, but in the early days he must be carried to ensure that he holds on until he gets there. If he 'poops' on the way and leaves a scent, he will probably do it again in the future. Male dogs will eventually, of course, raise their legs and pee at random to establish a territory, but if you can confine the stools to one area it is a great plus! Eventually you will be able to remove the wire netting as he gets into his toilet routine. Never leave your little dog alone in a wired-off area in case he tries to escape and gets caught up in the net.

Upon his first encounter with the inside of your house, it is always as well to restrict his territory to the kitchen, allowing quick and easy access to the garden, at least until he really feels settled and can extend his area of responsibility. It's no use allowing children to play with a new puppy in their bedroom and expecting him to be the pillar of virtue. When he needs to 'go' he will 'go', it's that simple. Children are not experienced enough to watch for the telltale signs, the uncomfortable behaviour, the sniffing and searching for a nice soft spot to use as a toilet. Often their attention is taken up by something else for a moment and the puppy has made his mark on the carpet in the corner, unnoticed. What a pity! Now he will most certainly try to go there again at his earliest opportunity and all your good intentions are blown.

Puppies are most certainly not children's toys and the younger members of the family must learn from the start to respect the fact.

House training

So here he is in his new home. Everything must seem very big and different to him. Hard to imagine really, just what the world looks like to a little chap of only eight or nine inches tall, or less! Why not try to see it from his point of view for a moment? If you lie on the carpet your head should be about on a level with his shoulders, depending of course upon his breed or type. You will be surprised how daunting it all seems from down there. Now maybe you will appreciate just why he jumps up to you at every opportunity. Your face and hands are the bits that communicate the most to him and they are an awfully long way up. So, whenever you want him to come to you, crouch down to his level and this way you won't be so intimidating. He will happily bound over because your face and hands are within his reach. *This simple tip is the rock solid basis for all of your training* – the way to always ensure that your dog will come back to you when he is called. The secret to it all is to try not to make a mistake in the first instance. Start off as you mean to continue. Coming to you must *always* be a happy experience.

Starting out on the right foot means getting your new arrival to understand a few basic rules from the beginning. The plain and simple word 'no' is your rock; the foundation upon which you will build your house. Let's face facts; we cannot expect to put a chimney onto the roof until we have assembled the building, brick by brick. 'No' is simple and precise and it should be used for *any* behaviour which you find undesirable – providing it is said at the *precise* moment the puppy or dog acts in a way which you find unacceptable, be it jumping onto furniture, chewing shoes, or whatever. But if you chastise several minutes *after* the event, all is lost, as his little brain will not be able to re-wind back to the action which took place a few minutes earlier and he will *associate* the reprimand with whatever he *is doing at the time*. This could possibly be a quite ordinary situation where perhaps he may be happily coming over to greet you. So it must be obvious that any chastisement given now will do damage and maybe even discourage the little fellow from coming to you as *he will think that he is doing wrong!* (See Association of Ideas, page 33.)

Some people believe that taking a puppy back to the 'scene of the crime' is sufficient, showing him his misdemeanour and even rubbing his nose in it. This is no use at all. You will only make matters worse. If he has pooped on the carpet now, ask yourself honestly, whose fault is it? It is certainly not his. You should have had him in a spot where you could keep an eye on him so you could whisk him out at the first telltale sign. But if you can actually catch him at the *precise* moment that he *tries* to go, which is the next step to the 'sniff and search for a spot' stage, then say 'no, no', grab him by the scruff and shake him up **just a little, like his Mum would do** and carry him as fast as you can to his spot in the garden. This is very effective! Do be careful, though: don't *over*-chastise or he may 'let loose' from fright. Just move in, lightning fast, tell him 'no' fairly and severely, scoop him up as fast as you can and get him outside.

This experience will do him a world of good as it will give him the opportunity to *associate* his actions with the 'no' command and he will realize that he has displeased you. He will soon learn that toilet outside generates praise and good positive vibrations and toilet *inside* just the opposite. Try to continue this way, watching constantly for the slightest indication that your puppy may need to relieve himself. He will, of course, always go immediately upon waking and just after eating, but don't imagine that these will be the only times that he will feel the urge! This is why it is so important to keep a new puppy within your sight the whole time. Mum is usually the one who ends up house-training because she spends the most time in the kitchen, but it should be the joint responsibility of **every member of the family** to keep an eye out for the first telltale signs. Watch out for that head down 'search and sniff' behaviour. Once a puppy's head goes down it is usually only a matter of a minute or so before he will actually 'let go', so it is up to everyone to keep their eyes peeled at all times.

You will be amazed at the speed with which a young puppy will fall into a routine if it is adhered to faithfully. He will soon make his own way to the door, indicating his wish to be let out, and can be completely house-trained (at least during the day) within a very short time. Night-time training will depend to a large extent upon the age of the puppy when you get it. If it is only eight weeks or so, then you must be prepared to take on the responsibility in exactly the same way as if a new human baby were to join the household.

Common-sense rules are:

1) Don't feed the last meal later than 6.30 p.m. and don't over-exercise at the end of the day, rendering him thirsty and encouraging him to drink large quantities. In fact, take up the water bowl by 6.00 p.m. until he is old enough to control himself.

   Some puppies do settle better after a small, light supper at around 10 p.m. but this will certainly mean that they will need to relieve themselves in the night. I personally have always opted to give the total daily requirements before 6.30 p.m. and have never had any problems in getting a little dog to settle down at night. The sooner they get into the routine of sleeping through the night, the better for all. But the choice is yours.

2) Make certain that he has done all he needs to do before you retire to bed (as late as possible).

3) Be prepared for him to wake early just as a human baby does. His little system can only hang on for a reasonable length of time, and it would be grossly unfair to severely chastise a puppy who had made a mess on the kitchen floor just because no member of the household was prepared to make the effort to get up early and let him out. The absolute *ideal* is to wake *before* him, which means rising at about 5.30/6.00 a.m. and putting him out *at once*! Then while he 'performs', make a cup of tea and go back to bed again. Don't be daft enough, of course, to feed or water him until the family is up and having breakfast at a more sociable hour.

Of course, by far the easiest way to 'night train' a puppy is to have it with you. No, I do *not* suggest it sleeps on the bed – far from it! But you can pop him into a nice secure travel box or cage (which will prove worth its weight in gold later when you go on holiday or do your own grooming – see chapter 8). Then all you need to do is to make him comfortable by your bed. He will be **reassured by your closeness** and you can talk to him until he settles. Then if he whimpers in the early hours, just pick him up straight from the box and carry him outside. *Don't* let him walk with you or he will try to go at the first opportunity. Once outside praise him 'in the act' and then fetch him back indoors and settle him down in the box again.

Simple and effective and *it works*! You will find that within only a few days all your splendid efforts will have paid off and he will sleep as a new baby does, a little longer each night, and that he will eventually waken at a socially acceptable time.

The big point to remember here is that no animal will foul its sleeping quarters unless it is sick or left for an unreasonable length of time, whereupon it may well become so distressed that it has no alternative. So, if you confine his area of responsibility to his box, his natural desire will be to keep it clean and he will let you know when he needs to go out. The box system of house training works extremely well and is beneficial in many ways.

One can, of course, opt just to leave the puppy in the kitchen in a dog bed and you may well be lucky, but the chances are that you are giving him too great an area of responsibility too soon! His bed will probably stay clean (providing of course that he sleeps in it when you are not there), but the kitchen floor covers a large space and he can leave his sleeping quarters and establish a toilet area elsewhere. This situation may also arise if the cage or crate you use is too large. He will sleep at one end and toilet at the other, thus going whenever he pleases and keeping his sleeping area clean at the same time, but not learning to control himself!

Some puppies are 'paper trained' when you get them, which means that they will trot over to a designated spot in the kitchen and toilet to order on the *Evening News*. This method suits many people and I will most certainly not decry it, but it does have drawbacks. 1) Paper is absorbent and the scent seeps through, leaving the floor beneath very tempting later. (No disinfectant will ever deceive the keen nose of a dog!) 2) One still has the task of actually *training* the dog to go outside, moving the paper nearer to the door each day and then eventually putting it into the garden.

Leaving paper in the kitchen overnight is an open invitation to the puppy to use it and not to 'hang on'. So the choice is yours. Paper training *does* work, but it takes longer and still has to be cleaned up each morning and, of course, is not very hygienic in the kitchen, particularly if there are very young children around who may play on the floor. So I opt for the cage or travel box every time as it is very effective, even though it does involve a bit more personal effort with regard to rising early in the beginning. But the fact remains that one can imprint a young dog's brain very easily into establishing a routine which will stand him in good stead for the rest of his life.

The cage or box may be transferred to the kitchen as soon as the puppy is sleeping through the night until an acceptable hour, and eventually (but don't rush it or you may take a step backwards) the door of the box may be left open and he will use it as his own spot, his personal retreat. Be scrupulously fair to him though, and never leave him shut in the box if you want a lie in.

What is nice about the crate system is that one can give a puppy some relief from the children during the day by just popping him in for an hour or so to rest, or just to keep him under control whilst you get on with day-to-day chores or answer the door or telephone. At least you know that he is safe and out of mischief. *Never use the crate as a punishment!* Let it be a haven, a spot of privacy all his own and he will grow to love it. It is all a matter of *association*.

My own dogs adore their crates as they have all been brought up with them and, in fact, Pippin is extremely protective of hers. The other dogs will happily swap and change boxes, but if one of them should happen to doze off in *hers* she will always know, and quite audibly snort with indignation and completely rearrange the blanket afterwards. I have actually seen her chuck the blanket out when someone else has dared to invade her territory – thus proving how much the box means to her. It is all a matter of how the situation is approached in the first place.

The crate is also a godsend for travelling and going on holiday. A dog is far safer riding in a car if he is contained in a crate or box. He must sit still and cannot jump around and cause distractions. Plus, in the unfortunate event of an accident, he is not able to dash out in panic in the face of oncoming traffic. The police have a high regard for responsible dog owners who ensure that in an emergency they have one item less to worry about!

As for going on holiday, I have lost count of the number of 'no dogs allowed' hotels who have let us in when they learned that the pet was to spend the night in a box. In fact, fairly recently one bed and breakfast landlady spent an evening in our room talking to the dog through the bars of the crate whilst we went out to dinner; completely won over to the system after almost throwing us out when she first learned that we had a pet in the car. Well worth a thought!

Before you put up your hands in horror at the thought of your pet spending the night in a confined space, think of it this way. Once he is asleep he really won't mind where he is actually situated, as long as he is warm and comfortable. I am assuming, of course, that you are prepared to get up nice and early to take him out for that brisk constitutional (it will do you both good!). Then just pop him back into his box or cage until you have eaten breakfast and off you go for the day.

Your landlady will love you for it and your dog won't mind a bit. He would rather sleep in a box with you close at hand than languish in kennels – I'm sure! It's the old story. If he *associates* his box with *good secure connotations* and he is *never left for an unreasonable length of time*, he won't object. I promise.

One last tip whilst we are on the subject of toilet training. It is always *most* useful to use a word or phrase whenever you put your puppy out to do his stuff. Anything will do, whatever suits you, but stick to it. We always say 'off you go', which is quite tasteful in non-doggie company, but 'do it here' would do just as well, or whatever takes your fancy. The fact is that the puppy will *associate* the phrase with the toilet action if it is used *every* time by *every member of the family*. The result of this effort will be an adult dog who will pee on command! What a joy when in a hurry or travelling. Remember to use the words when out walking, as soon as the puppy shows the inclination. This way he will go *on the lead*. Most useful when parked at a busy roadside cafe!

All good pals and jolly good company

Cats and dogs can live together in perfect harmony. It all depends upon how the matter is approached in the first place. Any dog who has had the house to himself for a year or so may resent an intruder. Likewise, a cat who has ruled supreme may take umbrage at the arrival of a puppy. Which way is best? To introduce a new kitten to an older dog or vice versa? It doesn't matter too much if you are sensible, although I prefer to introduce the kitten to the older dog. Adult cats can be very dangerous when upset by a lively puppy. Dogs seem more tolerant, as kittens are usually smaller than them and offer no threat.

It's all a question of socialization and here's where the good old cage method is worth its weight in gold once more. Do use a cage, not a travel box, to enable the kitten or puppy to view the new world from all four sides. You may already have a cage, but if not, don't lash out and buy one especially. Try to borrow one. Some vets have a few spare cages and for a small deposit could probably be persuaded to let one out on loan for a day or so, or try your local kennels. When your new kitten arrives home put her into the cage together with everything she requires. Newspaper, a nice cardboard box with a blanket, food and water bowls and a litter tray. Place the cage on top of the paper (if it doesn't have a floor) so the kitten won't scratch it up into a messy heap in the corner as she attends to her

'Getting to Know You'. The kitten, safe within the confines of the cage, is happy to make friends from behind the bars. After only twenty-four hours, the two should become 'best pals' (see back jacket). If the kitten has everything she requires she will come to no harm in that short space of time. The cardboard box is secured with a bungee strap to ensure that it does not tip and contains a comfortable blanket

toilet. When she is in and secure, let your dog into the room to meet the new arrival. Now don't have any conscience about putting the cat in a cage. You know that she has everything she needs and it's for her own good! When your dog gets close to the cage the kitten will probably hiss and spit (unless she has come from a household where dogs are kept). This will probably excite your dog who may adopt a play behaviour with his front end down on his elbows and his rear end up in the air, tail wagging with glee. Now just think what might have happened had the kitten not been in the cage. Utter chaos! It would probably have lashed out at the dog and taken flight, resulting in a chase which could wreck your living room in three minutes flat! Great sport, thinks the dog. Shock, horror, thinks the kitten. Mayhem rules supreme! Yippee!

If a kitten is kept within the confines of a cage for, say, twenty-four or even forty-eight hours, this will serve two purposes. 1) She will become accustomed to her new surroundings and will learn to tolerate the dog which offers no threat from the other side of the bars. 2) She will reinforce her litter training with excellent results as it is virtually impossible for her to make a mistake in such a small area. By the time you let her out she will trot to her tray in fine style. Most kittens are scrupulously clean, but not all! Some need a bit of extra encouragement.

Some dogs will dig around in cat litter, sniffing and spilling it all over the floor, sometimes even trying to eat the contents, litter and all. Ugh! Not a very nice habit and not to be tolerated. No-one knows for certain why they do this. It may be derived from some dim and distant instinctive origins, like muck-rolling. Thank goodness dogs that behave this way are few and far between. If you are unlucky and your dog does upset the apple cart, let him do it again; bait him back into the situation so your chastisement is both easy for him to understand and *fair*! Give him a severe correction at the *precise moment he starts to dig or eat the contents of the tray* to enable him to associate his actions with the word NO! Don't for heaven's sake be cruel! He is an animal doing (despite the fact that we don't understand why) what some animals consider to be natural, but he must learn that his actions are against your wishes. The ideal situation is to put the litter tray in a spot where the dog is not allowed and if in the future your cat learns to toilet outside, your troubles should be over. Please remember though, he *is not a bad dog*. Just a natural, instinctive animal who must learn to adapt to a lifestyle which we consider to be acceptable and which may require quite a bit of adjustment on his part. He will learn, I promise!

The whole situation will be reversed if you introduce a puppy to an older cat and it's most certainly in the puppy's interest to cage him for at least twenty-four hours in the room where your cat spends the most time.

This may well avert a fracas which the cat would undoubtedly win, with the possibility of nasty, painful consequences for the puppy.

Just keep everything low key and gently introduce the pair over a period of time. Neither a puppy nor a kitten will come to any harm in a cage for a day or so and in the case of the puppy, house training will be so much easier for him to learn. As you remove him every hour or so to carry him outside (see section on house training, page 18), by the time you eventually let him out to meet his new pal and explore, your job will be half done.

With time and patience the end result will be a lifetime of friendship between the two. All my animals live in harmony and share their food. The cats rub against the dogs and, on odd occasions, sleep with them. Great buddies all.

The photograph of Pippin holding the kitten in the sock (page 113) demonstrates perfect harmony between two animals. Despite the fact that the baby is inches away from Pippin's jaws, she remains trusting and contented. The photo took only a matter of minutes to take and no stress was put upon either animal. It was all a matter of preparation (see section on photography, page 108). Everything was set to go. Lights were checked and camera focused. Pippin was asked to 'sit' and 'stay'. The baby was quite content to be tucked into a nice soft, warm sock and then Pippin was asked to 'hold'. The baby, as one can easily see in the picture, remained relaxed and happy for a matter of about two and a half minutes. She was fascinated with the camera and consequently stared at it with interest. Magic! Once the photograper Arthur Sidey, was certain that he had the shot he wanted the sock was gently removed from Pippin's mouth (she wasn't allowed to *drop* it of course!) and the baby went off to play with her litter mates. This is pure compatibility between animals and it is demonstrated even more strongly in the shot of Max with the ducklings (see page 114). They were warm and cosy nestling against his fur (one even dozed off) and Max, gentle giant that he is, just gazed at them in fascination (one of my all-time favourite photos). With understanding and infinite patience creatures great and small of any species, size or colour will learn to live together in harmony. Here lies a lesson for us all!

Incidentally, the kitten in the sock eventually went on to her new home – a household with a dog.

She is blissfully happy.

Note

These photos were set up by professionals under strictly controlled conditions. The amateur should not attempt such advanced situations but should rather concentrate on single animals or genuine 'best pals' who are brought up together.

Love thy neighbour

What a subject! More love is lost between neighbours over furry friends than is lost over almost any other situation. Many a good relationship goes down the drain when one of the parties acquires a dog. Let's face it, just because we ourselves are animal-lovers, it doesn't necessarily follow that Mr and Mrs Joe Soap next door have to be also.

Before you even consider taking delivery of a new puppy, make absolutely certain that the garden is secure. Young puppies get great sport from wriggling through small gaps in the fence and visiting the next garden, especially if there are children out there, voicing encouragement. A bored puppy will look around for amusement and will certainly take advantage of any small break in the hedge or fence in order to explore the outside world. Let us suppose our neighbour is a keen gardener. Little Fido doesn't know this, or care! All he is interested in is a good game and a dig in the vegetable patch, or even a super bonker dog dash all over the newly seeded lawn (much more fun than pottering around in his own garden). Lots of new and exciting smells to investigate. The result of this escapade can be very unpleasant. Mr Soap is quite within his rights to complain bitterly and if the situation is repeated often he could possibly choose to take legal action.

Oh my! What a pity. Just as we had all been getting along so nicely. Live and let live is the answer to this. Mr Soap is entitled to his peace and quiet and a tidy garden, just as we are entitled to keep a nice well-behaved, controlled pet. Anyone can make the odd mistake and if it is dealt with in a reasonable fashion no-one will mind too much. However, if your dog *does* dig up your neighbour's flowers, accept your responsibilities; don't meet anger with anger as this will only inflame the situation.

The humble apology usually cures all, coupled with your promise to see that the little rascal will stay on his own territory in future. A good secure fence and a shut gate would, of course, have avoided the whole problem. Don't be proud. If it is your fault, admit it! Apologize and that should be the end of the matter. Life is too short for aggravation.

A barking dog is usually a bored dog. A bored dog is more often than not a destructive dog. A digger and fence-jumper. If you work full-time, it is unthinkable to leave a dog shut up in the house for possibly ten hours a day, so you must consider leaving it in the garden. The only safe way to do this is to construct a cement-based run with strong fencing and ideally a cover or roof. The top may be made of chain link, or better still, corrugated plastic to keep your pet clean and dry. A warm comfortable kennel or box should be provided and a supply of fresh drinking water.

These conditions will be more than adequate for the physical requirements of your dog (providing, of course, that you are prepared to keep the run in a clean and hygienic state). However, they will do little for his psychological well being. Dogs, if left alone for long periods on a regular basis, develop many behavioural problems, one of the worst being constant barking. I have known dogs under such conditions develop throat problems through barking and howling continuously for hours or even days on end!

Some dogs may well stop when they hear their owners return home and it is even remotely possible for them to be unaware of the problem; hardly likely though as they will probably receive complaints from their neighbours. What can one do? Well, one member of the family could consider working part time, or one could get the pet a companion: another dog, ideally of the opposite sex, spayed or neutered (so as to offer neither an invitation nor a threat). This can go a long way towards relieving the situation, as can making the supreme effort and getting up as much as an hour earlier each day and taking him out, not for a potter and pee, but for a darned good run! This, coupled with a hefty meal upon returning, should settle him down at least for four hours or so.

A dog with a full stomach is far more likely to rest than one who is pacing the floor looking forward to his evening meal. So if you *must* leave your dog or dogs out during the day, feed in the mornings just before you leave. Makes sense. Don't, of course, feed any dog if you intend leaving it for several hours *indoors*. The results could be disastrous and no fault of the animal's. House pets are best fed in the evenings.

I personally feel that it is unfair to keep a dog if one works full-time. But if you *do*, then you must accept the responsibility, and endeavour to make his life as pleasant as possible. Remember too that when you arrive home 'whacked' after a hard day, he will be raring to go! Are you prepared to get off your rear end and take him out? If not, you shouldn't have him.

3

Bare necessities

Every dog has certain basic requirements which should be provided at the outset: a bed, bowls, a collar and lead.

The bed

It is extremely important for a dog of any age to have a place to call his own. The crate discussed in the previous chapter is perfect as it affords privacy and protection from all sides, but it is not a very desirable item in the living room as it probably won't fit in with the decor. A pet bed or basket of a suitable size is very nice but one need not lash out lots of money in order to give one's dog a suitable rest place. In the case of tiny dogs, a washing-up bowl will do very well if lined with a piece of blanket, or the perfect alternative is the cardboard box! This can be placed in any quiet corner and if it happens to be a bit ugly (perhaps over-printed with 'beer' or 'baked beans') it can be secreted behind a sofa. Cheap and cheerful and your dog will love it! Once he has learned 'STAY' (see chapter 5) all you have to do is point to his bed and use whatever command you find suitable. 'Bed', 'Basket' or 'Box' would do, and if necessary place him into it first so that he understands and then say 'stay'. He will soon learn to appreciate the fact that he has a place of his own. It is also the ideal store for all his personal treasures – his half-eaten chew sticks, squeaky toys and the like. Pippin, star that she is, still sleeps in a humble cardboard box by the sofa and hides all her goodies under the blanket.

The travel and sleeping crate has a final use – probably one which will please Mum the most! If it is kept in the porch or just inside the kitchen door, lined with old towels, it is an absolute godsend when your dog comes in after walking in filthy weather. Once inside, he can 'shake, rattle and roll', rub himself clean and remain there for about twenty minutes or so,

'A place of my own' – little Holly in her 'posh bed'

'Home 'n' Dry'. A great game in the snow then straight into the cage for a good 'shake, rattle and roll'. After just a few minutes a good brisk rub down with the towel and the dog is in a fit state to be allowed indoors again. If the weather is very cold, don't leave a wet dog for too long in an outside porch. A short spell in the cage will absorb the worst and ensure that your carpets stay clean and dry

after which time he should emerge dry enough to be allowed back into the house. Just think of it! No muddy wet tails wagging and sloshing black marks all over the fridge door and no filthy feet on the kitchen floor. Remember to remove the wet towels, though, or they will soon smell! By the morning the shed mud will have dried in the crate and reduced down to a powder which can be vacuumed out of the box. Far better in your Hoover than all over the carpets.

It is the little irritations which can build up to enormous proportions, when people buy dogs without giving any thought to the possibilities of filthy paws, or hair on the furniture, often ending with the pet having to go through no fault of his own. So for everyone's sake (his in particular), keep Mum sweet-tempered and don't let him back indoors until he is clean and dry. The crate will serve this purpose beautifully!

The collar

Collars on puppies are a necessary evil. Necessary because a dog *must* carry identification and evil because they can be dangerous, particularly to a lively youngster ever searching for mischief. We quite happily put elastic collars onto kittens but never imagine for a moment that a puppy could strangle himself with a leather one. The fact is that it can happen and I speak from bitter experience.

I returned home after being out for only a very short time, leaving a puppy together with another little dog for company, 'safe' and 'secure' in a pen at the bottom of the garden. On my return I called out to them as usual and when only the little dog replied, I went down to find the puppy hanging by his collar from a tree branch that had poked through the fence, just low enough for him to get caught on as he put his feet up to see out. Now this is a chance happening with odds at I don't know how many million to one against, but nevertheless it happened to me and I feel so strongly about it that I pass on this experience for what it is worth.

The fact is that if the collar had been elastic he would have been able to free himself as his body weight stretched it. The irony of this sad story is that the collar and identity disc had only been put on him that very morning as a precaution because there was some building work in progress at the back of my property and I was being prepared for any eventuality: such as the off-chance that the digger-operator may have caught the fence, causing damage and allowing the dogs to escape.

Whenever you feel you must leave your puppy unattended, try to find a cat collar which fits him and use that. If his neck is too big, ask your local leather shop or saddler to insert a bit of stretch material, rubber, or strong elastic into one that is large enough. After all, it *is* only to carry identification in case he gets lost and nothing more, so why take a chance? In fact, any young dog could quite happily trot around with his identity disc hanging on a length of strong elastic. Just make sure it is exactly the right size; not big enough to slip over his head and not tight enough to be uncomfortable. Remembering, of course, how fast puppies grow. Anything worn round the neck *must* of course be checked daily without fail.

The sight of my little dog hanging there will be with me forever and it took many months before I would even talk about it to anyone. I felt responsible. I should have noticed the branch and didn't, so I just hope that in writing this some other puppy may be saved from the same fate.

Choke chain collars, of course, are *deadly* and should *never* be left on a dog of any age. At the kennels where I worked in Hollywood any trainer who returned a dog to its run with a chain around its neck would be dragged over hot coals, and if it happened a second time the person responsible would lose his or her job. Choke chain collars are lethal if they get caught and my hair stands on end every time I see a dog running loose with one around its neck, especially if it carries an identity disc, indicating that it is probably worn all the time!

Which collar to use for walking and training? There are many styles of leading devices on the market and the one you choose will depend upon the size, shape and temperament of your dog. There is no one perfect design which suits all. Puppies, if started young, really only require gentle persuasion and if trained properly should need no more than that for the rest of their lives. (This is why I favour a soft slip collar.) Adults vary so much that it may require a bit of experimentation before finding a suitable method.

Choke chains, leads and halters

One will always come across the pro 'choke chainers' and the anti 'chokers'. Many people favour a new headstall method of control, which I believe originated in America and is now being developed over here. It is really quite simply a case of 'horses for courses'.

If used intelligently the choke chain collar is ideal for strong, thick-necked dogs and there can be no doubt that the 'clink' of the links can do a great deal to reinforce the correction when the dog is checked. It is really the most popular method when training a dog to walk at 'close' heel for competition purposes, and not at all cruel if used properly – the *right* way round! The chain collar should immediately slacken on release.

The headstall or halter style suits many people who own dogs with long, pointed faces. Many of the larger breeds fit the bill here (Setters and the like). This method of control is fine if you just require your dog to walk in a comfortable fashion. You will never quite get the same 'precision' using a halter, but it is more than adequate for a non-competitive dog. Both have drawbacks; nothing is perfect.

As for leads, I personally go for the finest lightest leather lead I can find, giving the maximum sensitivity and 'feel'. The larger dogs possibly need heftier leads but I still always go for leather, soft and strong. Chain leads are nowhere near as pleasant to hold and control. Expandable lines – well what can I say? They are very nice for the owners who feel that little Fido is getting a lot more exercise on the end of his nice long line. The fact that little Fido is still walking at *exactly* the same pace as his owner despite the fact that he is ten feet ahead seems to go unnoticed. The total lack of sensitivity in a box of plastic must surely be obvious and my biggest criticism is the fact that dogs on these lines are encouraged to pull. They would also be extremely difficult to control in a fight situation where one needed to make an *instant* move in order to forcibly remove one's pet from the affray. They are a bit of a novelty and there *is* a place for them in the Christmas stocking, but they are more for the owner's wellbeing than the dog's. They could, however, be quite useful in the park if one were to remain on the spot and allow one's pet 'freedom' in a wide circle. Ideal for the 'naughty' little dog who won't come back when he is called unless attached. (But he still cannot walk any faster than his owner when on the street, be he twenty feet in front!)

4

Leading off

In discussing training throughout this book we are following the progress of a dog from the puppy stage, but the methods described will also work well with adults! Old habits die hard, of course, and it may take a little longer with an older dog, but the secret of all animal training is to try to see it their way. Have patience. Try to think what it would be like if a member of some 'superior' species were to inflict their wishes upon you! You may take kindly to the situation if approached in an acceptable fashion, but if, on the other hand, you were to get the rough end of the bargain, you might rebel and who could blame you? Think about it!

Dogs and indeed most, if not all, animals understand positive and negative or black and white. Shades of grey tend to confuse, so bold and positive praise proffered *instantly* is extremely effective; reinforced, if necessary, with a treat of some kind. It is not vital to give a reward but some dogs, especially greedy ones, do respond to the added reinforcement of food. There is no hard and fast rule – just whatever it takes! One can usually refrain from using tit bits as soon as the animal understands clearly and exactly what one is asking for and it is willing to co-operate.

Association of ideas

To associate a word, a scent, a sound or a visible action with a certain situation is basically the limit of your dog's intelligence. Bless the heart of the dear little old lady who will tell you that her doggie understands 'every word she says', because of course this is not possible. Although some dogs do learn to associate with a larger vocabulary as they develop, even to the point of *seeming* to understand each word, these are the smart ones who can listen and pick out the single sounds incorporated into a human sentence which they connect with certain commands or actions. The old lady will argue that at feeding time, she calls him in a different manner each day, using a string of mixed sentences and he *always* comes bounding up with his tail wagging. What she doesn't realize, is that unconsciously she is doing something with regularity that the dog is associating with food and it is *that* action or sound which brings him running. It could be the click of the cupboard door as she opens it to reach for the can, or the sound of the can opener, or again, possibly her regular pattern of movements at one particular time of day. What it most certainly is *not* is the garbled mixture of words that she is uttering, although *tone* of voice can play a part.

Verbal commands are an integral part of the domestic dog's life, but they must be simple and precise, to enable him to *associate* the word with a certain action. If you say, for example, 'Don't jump up onto the chair you naughty boy' in an admonishing voice, you *may* get a reaction purely on the verbal *tone*, but you probably won't get any response from the sentence if uttered in a normal or cheerful voice.

It is good to get him to *associate* with several simple words from the beginning. The most important being a straightforward NO. (No frills, just NO!) Let him associate this word given in a stern tone with *anything* that you do not wish him to do. The one mistake many new puppy owners make is to say the word 'down' and 'go down' when he jumps up on to furniture, people etc. 'DOWN' is a command which he will learn later and it has an entirely different significance, so let it suffice to use the word 'NO' for *anything* that is forbidden, coupled (if necessary) with a little just and fair chastisement. He can then associate with the word and know that his actions are against your wishes.

If, on the other hand, you wish him to go into the down position, the ideal situation is first 'NO!' because his actions (whatever they are) are undesirable, then in a pleasant tone give the *down* command. He will soon learn the difference if you keep your instructions simple.

You don't have to wait until your puppy is old enough for training classes to begin his education. Almost any child who has attended a kindergarten or play-group will find settling in at school later on so much easier. He or she will have become accustomed, in a pleasant fashion, to the general educational environment, even though actual lessons are not taught. The child will accept a bit of organization from the play-group leader and learn to give and take. This can only do good and the experience will doubtless give him the edge over his less fortunate classmates when the big day arrives! There are no kindergartens for puppies, so it is up to us to try to steer them along the right path from the start.

The type of training and socialization in this book will be more than sufficient for the average family pet, but if you wish to attend classes at a later date when your puppy is around six months old, fine! None of the behaviours demonstrated here will clash with anything you may be taught at obedience school later. The classes will be great experience for your little friend and will go a great way in helping him to get along with other dogs. The lessons he has learned will stand him in good stead.

It is often the case that dog-owners attend classes just to *cure* bad habits which may have already developed into problems (mostly pulling), and it is also often the case that dogs may well walk nicely round a ring in a church hall (where really they have little opportunity to do anything else) and then when the owners get them home it's 'Look out chaps! Here we go again. Tug-of-war time. Yippee!' So if you can spare a few minutes a day from the *start*, from the moment your puppy is able to go out onto the streets, the chances are that he will never develop any naughty behaviours, only common sense!

A line of communication

So now here is the big day. All vaccinations complete and we are ready to start training. Decision time! Who is going to be the boss? Him or you? Make your mind up NOW, and don't think that just because you own a small breed of puppy that it doesn't matter too much if he pulls a bit (after all, he's not going to yank your arms out like a mastiff would). *Of course* it matters! It matters even if he is a Yorkshire Terrier! There is nothing worse than seeing a dog at full stretch, hacking and coughing with the strain, its owner in tow, not able to relax for a moment, arms outstretched and trying desperately to control the animal. What a miserable existence and totally unnecessary. A dog should be a pleasure to walk, at any size. You should be able to relax and enjoy a conversation with a friend or just take in the view without having to be constantly checking or having your arm pulled out of its socket. Dogs must *always* be on a lead on the public highway. In many areas this is the law! Even if it were not, it is very undesirable to walk a dog, even on quiet back roads, without one. You should always be prepared for the unexpected.

I refuse to accept the excuses I hear from people who may have obtained a few prizes at obedience shows, saying, 'My dog is so well trained he doesn't need a lead', or 'My dog would *never* run away from me'. Given the right (or wrong) set of circumstances, he does and he would! *No dog is totally predictable off the lead. Natural instincts will always take over from trained behaviours* if he is faced with the unexpected. Suppose, for example, that someone has left their front gate open and their nasty, fiery pet dashes out onto the street ready to take on the world. Your innocent dog (if off the lead) would be enticed into a fight situation in seconds and this could result in a chase which might possibly end with one or both dogs getting killed under a car; not to mention putting the life of the motorist at risk. Think about it! Most dogs will chase wildlife; rabbits, squirrels and the like, and a large number will run after cats.

One cannot control where a dog will toilet if he is off the lead. At least if you can guide him into the gutter to do his stuff it will prevent him from fouling the public walkway – (a serious offence). One hopes also, of course, that you will make every effort to dispose of the evidence afterwards – wherever he does it.

Now that we have established the reasons why a dog should always be on the lead, how do we go about it? Not difficult really. No magic. No hard and fast rules either. As dogs, like children, are all different, where one may benefit from gentle handling another may respect a slightly tougher approach. There are many ways to approach the situation, depending upon the breed, size, type and disposition of your dog. But there *are* two very simple and no-nonsense rules: 1) to pull is uncomfortable and undesirable, and 2) to walk nicely at your side is decidedly *more* comfortable and *very* desirable. Simple. So to begin.

We must have a suitable method of controlling the puppy and, as explained in the previous chapter, we have to decide upon the type of collar used. I like a slip collar based on the choke chain design but made of softer material, either rope or nylon 'tape', but a metal choke chain will do just as well and it does have a nice 'clink' to it, allowing the puppy to *associate* the correction with the sound and it can sometimes help to reinforce the exercise.

If your puppy is very 'soft' a leather collar should suffice. Whichever method you choose, it really won't be all that important at the beginning as we merely want to get the little fellow used to being confined to the end of a lead. It's not a bad idea to put a collar onto a young puppy and then attach a lead and let him drag it around for a while (don't ever leave him alone of course, in case he gets it tangled). Try this in the garden a couple of times before you pick up the other end and encourage him to walk with you.

As soon as you do take up the lead and attempt to get the puppy to follow he will probably plonk his rear end down and refuse to budge. He will resent the tension, so relax and get down to his eye level and call him to you, holding the end of the lead. When he approaches, make a fuss of him and then stand up and try again. He *may* take to it like a duck to water, but the chances are that he will pull back or sit down.

This early stage in the basic training takes love and patience as it will be his first encounter with discipline. The first time in his life when he must learn that he can't have everything his own way. So in order that we don't build up any resentment we must be gentle. Jolly him along a bit, encouraging him to follow you. Don't worry at this stage which side he is on, just keep on bending down to his level and encouraging him. He may trot with you as he gains confidence or he may pull back. If he does pull back, he may even yelp and struggle as he feels the restriction around his neck. Always release the tension and bend down and try to encourage him to follow you. If necessary even offer him a biscuit or something tasty just to get him going. Five or ten minutes of this should be sufficient for the first lesson. Always end any training session with a happy association, be it a game with a ball or just lots of praise – anything which may appeal to him as a reward for trying. This will impart the idea that training is a pleasant experience with something to look forward to at the end.

Before we go one step further, I must mention that there is a right and a wrong way to put on a slip or choke collar. I use a slip rope collar because it doesn't damage the hair (the majority of my dogs are shaggy or

In the pictures the puppy is to be walked on the left of the owner, so the top of the slip or choke is uppermost allowing a quick and kind release after checking. If the puppy is to be walked on the right then the situation must be reversed

long-coated). As I've said, a metal choke is perfectly all right if you prefer it. In fact, on some of the thick-necked, heavier breeds it is desirable. Now, having decided on which side we wish the puppy to walk, we will fit the collar accordingly. The picture illustrates quite clearly that the top of the ring must be uppermost on the side you wish your dog to walk (and *that* decision is entirely yours – see chapter 5).

If the collar is fitted correctly it will drop and release immediately after you have checked it. If it is put on the other way it will remain in the 'choke' position and will do just that – CHOKE – and achieve *nothing* because what we are aiming at is a situation whereby when the dog pulls he is uncomfortable and when he doesn't, he isn't. It's that simple! If the collar is on the wrong way it will still be uncomfortable *after the dog has corrected himself* and ceased to pull. Consequently he will be very confused. It's just a matter of common sense. Try slipping the choke collar over your wrist first in one position and then in the other. When you jerk sharply you will see and *feel* the difference immediately.

Between your puppy's ears there is an incredible computer, commonly known as a brain. Now as we go along, step by step, we will programme this computer and imprint behaviours, which will remain there for the rest of his life. At an early age he will soak up learning like blotting paper and you will be absolutely amazed at his capabilities. It is possible for you to produce a dog to be proud of, one with immaculate manners who will be a pleasure to own. You can do this with little effort but a great deal of common sense. Over the years I have become accustomed to people telling me how lucky I am to own such smart and intelligent animals – never a thought for the fact that they may well be just ordinary dogs which are highly educated.

All you will need to achieve similar success is to have infinite patience and empathy with your dog. He isn't human and he has to learn to adapt to your lifestyle. He must abide by the basic rules in exchange for his comfortable, loving environment. It isn't much to ask of him. But most important of all is that each exercise must be a pleasure for you both.

Now to begin. Let us assume that your puppy has become accustomed to wearing his choke or leather collar (whichever style you have decided upon for lead walking) and he will trot behind you in the garden for a step or two. Carry him out into the street and place him on the side which is the most comfortable for you and remember *always* to check that the choke is in the correct position. Now take a few steps and encourage him to trot alongside. After you have gone, say four or five paces, STOP. A sharp, *dead stop*. Tell him instantly to STAY. Now what we are aiming to achieve here is to imprint in his little brain that whenever you stop he must also. The element of surprise works wonders as it teaches him from the

After checking to see that the choke or slip collar is in the safe and kind position we are ready to go

Take just a few steps forward and chat away to your puppy keeping his attention. (This is very evident in the photo.) Step, say just one, two, three, four, five, and then come to an abrupt halt, a DEAD STOP. Now if you have only taken a few steps your puppy should not have had the opportunity to forge ahead and when you stop he will be quite surprised! Don't worry about his position at this stage; he may sit or stand as long as he takes notice and associates your actions with the word 'STAY' – say this clearly and precisely!

start that he can't daydream, he must pay attention! He isn't too young to *associate* the action of stopping with the verbal command and the hand signal demonstrated in the photograph on page 40 (*left*). In fact, the sooner he learns this, the better. To have a rock solid 'stay' is invaluable. So here we go!

Now show him a clear signal so he will have no opportunity to become confused. The stay signal is the flat hand held in a position where it can easily be seen. Repeat 'Fido stay' then quietly reassure him with 'staaay . . . that's good . . . stay'. Then after about twenty or thirty seconds, 'Fido heel' and off we go again. If you have to bend down to reassure him this is fine in the beginning, but once he gets the hang of things, you may remain upright. Just gain his confidence a bit at a time and relax! (This will help him no end.) It takes courage to use a loose lead in the beginning as one's natural instinct is to hold on tightly. It will only have an adverse effect if you do. Take heart, just communicate with your voice and your light line and it will work well for both of you

Little Holly (above right) is also trotting along in fine style. Note that as she is on my left, I am holding the slack 'line of communication' in my right hand, leaving my left one free on the off chance that I may have to make a correction. If your puppy is walking on the right, reverse the situation

Step one, two, three, four, five, chatting away and jollying him along, keeping his attention and possibly saying 'Fido heel. He-e-e-e-l. That's good. Good! STAY.' As you stop, bend down and stroke him and gently encourage him to 'sta-a-a-y'. 'That's good' (quietly does it). Remember that 'good' is only a *reinforcement* and it should not mean that the exercise is over. When you have managed to keep him in one spot for a few seconds, then choose a nice short release word, such as 'O.K.' and off we go again. 'Fido heel', step one, two, three, four, five (maybe six, seven and eight). STOP DEAD. 'Sta-a-y. Good. That's good. Sta-ay.' Keep your voice down. There's no need to shout at him like a sergeant major on the parade ground. 'Sta-a-a-y. Good. O.K.' And off we go again.

At this point it really doesn't matter what position he is in when he stops and stays. We will teach him to sit later on. Just keep on taking a few steps and then stop abruptly and give loads of gentle *quiet* encouragement to stay in the one spot until released.

Now, this exercise serves two purposes. One is that if performed correctly it will, without doubt, imprint the word and action of *stay* into his computer without putting any mental or physical pressure on the little fellow, and two, he cannot get into the habit of pulling *because you are not taking enough steps to allow the situation to develop.*

If the puppy is *never* allowed to pull from the start (because he is never given the opportunity to try) the chances are that when his training is over he will walk beautifully to heel. The act of pulling will be unknown. I repeat that the element of surprise keeps him on his toes as he *must* watch and listen, or he may get caught out as you stop suddenly. If his concentration lapses for a moment he will soon be jolted out of his reverie when you halt and the surprise will do him good. It won't hurt him in any way to experience a bit of *gentle* correction right away.

Don't worry too much about showing him the hand signal just yet. You may well require both hands as you stroke and steady him into the stay situation. The hand signal will come next. Just practise this exercise for, say, five minutes, two or three times a day for a week and by the end of that period (or even sooner) you will be *amazed* at how your little friend has learned to associate the stop action with the word 'stay' and will halt with you each time.

When we acquire a puppy it is very similar to when a baby arrives on the scene. There is much excitement and pride in the new arrival and also the feeling that *your* baby must do everything before everyone else's. How often do you hear proud mothers saying 'He is standing in his cot at eight months' or 'We are encouraging him to take his first steps at a year'. Each Mum, deep down, feels she has the best baby in the world and, of course, for her this is true! The point of all this is that it doesn't matter *how* long your puppy takes to develop as long as it is steady progress and an enjoyable experience for him. The hardest thing for a dog trainer to fight is his or her own ego! (And I'm as guilty as the rest.) The ONE MORE TIME syndrome *must* be fought *at all costs*. Five minutes per session is enough for a puppy's first week of training, always ending, as I said earlier, by some sort of happy experience like a game or maybe a nice meal.

If you push it too far you will have lost his concentration and that can be disastrous. Remember it is really all psychology. He *must* associate the exercise with a pleasant experience or all your efforts will be wasted and you must *always* quit when you are winning. Remember the common sense we mentioned earlier. Think about it for a moment. The last exercise he has performed at each session is **the one which will remain in his mind**, so it must be a good one! I understand only too well when one's animal has performed superbly in training, how easy it is to ask him to do it 'one more time'. It's such a thrill when you appear to be making a breakthrough. But, if the next time you ask him, he is not quite so good (or even no good at all) then if this is the last exercise of the day he will go to bed remembering that he has got off lightly! If you try to force him back to his earlier excellence it may take many attempts and could cultivate resentment and boredom. So swallow your pride and quit on a winner. This rule applies from day one!

5

Manoeuvres

After a week of 'stepping and stopping' your puppy should be steady enough to control with your 'lead' hand, allowing your other hand the freedom to show him the 'stay' signal (see picture below). Do place your hand in a position where he can see it clearly. If you chat away to him and keep his attention he should look up in your direction and take notice (this is clearly illustrated – the puppy was sixteen weeks at the time the photo was taken).

Now we will move on to stage two, *'stepping and turning'*. This will be the major factor in preventing your little friend from pulling as he *must* keep an eye on you at all times in order to anticipate what is coming next. Keep him on his toes; don't ever give him the chance to pull ahead. What he has never known he will never miss. Now step out and keep changing patterns in any order. *Don't establish a routine at all costs.*

Now, if we extend our training sessions to say ten to fifteen minutes, twice a day, we will have enough time to include a few new manoeuvres. *Example:* 'Fido heel! Heeeeel! Good. 'That's good.' Step one, two, three, four, five, 'STAY'. Stay stock still next to him and show him the hand signal. 'STAAY. That's good. Good. O.K.' And off we go again. 'Fido heel!' Step one two three four five. RIGHT TURN (90 degrees). Call him to you. 'Fido heel.' Step one, two, three, four, five. 'Good. That's good. STAY!' Stop again, showing a clear hand signal and then when you start off the next time, take a few steps forward in a straight line (never enough steps to give him the chance to get ahead of you) then *left about* turn (180 degrees) and keep on chatting. 'Fido heel, heel. That's good. Good.' Take say five or six more steps and 'STAY'. Stop stock still and 'stay' again with the signal and if he has performed well release him after about thirty seconds, drop down to his level and praise.

This exercise is magic if performed correctly and I do recommend that until you really have a good mutual understanding of the situation, you don't actually 'take him for a walk'. It's well worth two or three weeks out of his ten to fourteen years' life expectancy to get your act together. Get to know one another and build up a relationship first.

Within a few days your little friend will have become accustomed to walking with you in a nice comfortable fashion in any direction for short distances, with a sprinkling of 'stays' thrown in for good measure. When you feel confident that you have a mutual understanding, then take him off for a little walk around the block. Talk to him all the time, reassuring him if he is a bit traffic shy. This will soon be overcome as he gets accustomed to his new environment.

As there are no set rules with a pet puppy regarding which side he walks, it is a good idea to keep him near the wall, away from the noise (at least at first). Once you start taking your little dog for regular walks you are faced with the pee and poop situation! Puppies cannot hold on for long and will go as soon as they get the urge, so watch out for the telltale signs. He may suddenly stop and start to squat. Get him into the gutter or anywhere away from the public walkway, and let him finish. Then do your best to dispose of the evidence. As he actually 'performs' remember to use your chosen word (as we mentioned in the section on house training) to imprint the behaviour into his computer. *Do this every time without fail.*

While we are on the subject, don't allow the 'potter and pee' syndrome to develop – the bad habit of just going for the sake of it! Adult males will want to stop every few yards and make their mark. This really isn't necessary; it's just a nuisance, in fact it can grow and develop in exactly the same way as the irritating child's pony who has been allowed to stop every few yards to eat grass. Once established it is very hard to break the habit. I often see folks taking their pets for 'walks' and, in fact, all they are out for is a slow amble, a sniff and a pee, neither party getting any exercise whatsoever. They may just as well have spent the time in their armchair at home, letting their dog potter and pee in the back garden.

Once you are sure that he has done enough to satisfy the calls of nature, then just keep on at a nice brisk pace and don't allow too many stops. Do, of course, let him have one final go just before he goes back into the house, to be on the safe side. Puppies of course do require much more consideration until they can control themselves.

A few dos and don'ts on lead walking:

1) *Do* always try to keep your lead loose. This is very evident in all the photos. If a puppy is walking in the correct position there is no need to 'string him up'. He must learn that walking next to you is a comfortable and pleasant experience.

Remember, 'keep a nice loose lead at all times'

2) *Do* give a short sharp (but kind) check on the choke or slip collar if he tries to get ahead, or not turn when you want him to. *Don't* pull his head off! Just a quick gentle jerk and instant release, coupled with loads of verbal encouragement each time you change direction. Try just the words first. 'Fido, heel' if he isn't paying enough attention, then again 'Fido, HEEL'. Check (release) and off we go again. 'Good. That's good!' The more you keep on changing direction the less chance there is of him getting ahead. He *must* pay attention to you or he will get caught out. Please *don't* for a moment think that this sort of training is tough for a young puppy. Far from it. We are only talking of about five to fifteen minutes, twice a day and the experience will be invaluable. It's just a case of acclimatization; getting your youngster into good habits from the start. He can be a normal playful puppy for the remaining $23\frac{1}{2}$ hours of each day. The fact is that when the lead goes on he must learn from the absolute beginning that there are a few basic rules.
a) Lead on in the street; walk nicely and learn a few manners. (Can't be bad!)
b) Lead off at home; relax.

3) *Don't*, for heaven's sake, let a young child take him out onto the street for exercise. If you *do*, you may just as well not bother to spend time trying to train him. Children will let puppies get away with murder on the lead. They will run wild, allow them to stop at will, pee anywhere, and pull whenever the fancy takes them. I'm very fond of children and have two of my own, but when they were young they were never allowed to take the dogs out alone. They were, of course, able to hold on to them and walk with me, learning as they went along the full responsibility of dog ownership, but I never let them out ALONE with a puppy on the lead. Playing together in the garden, of course, is another story! This helps to establish a bond between them and build up a good relationship.

The sit

Our puppy is now trotting along in fine style and stopping whenever we ask him to. (Always at every kerb of course, for the sake of road safety.) So now we can teach him to sit. If you have set your sights upon obedience competitions in the future, you can incorporate the sit behaviour into your initial training and this will be fine for you. I don't teach the sit myself until I have thoroughly imprinted the stay. I like to get this into the computer in as simple a way as possible, with no chance of confusion. In many cases young dogs sit automatically when you stop. This is fine too,

To teach the sit. Take a few steps forward with your dog at your side and then come to a nice sharp 'stay'. This will get your student's attention, particularly if you keep communicating with him, 'Fido stay', 'that's good', etc. Now gently press his rear end into the sit position with your left hand, holding the lead loosely with your right one. Reassure him with the words 'sit' and 'stay' – 'Fido sit, that's good, now staaay'

Reassure him again and then slowly stand up. Don't make a quick move or you may unsettle him, and repeat 'Fido sit, that's good, now staaay'. Show him a nice clear stay signal (remember your loose line at all times). If he gets up just put him back into the correct position and try again. Do not get frustrated with him if he doesn't grasp it right away. The more relaxed you are with the situation the more confidence you will instil into your student. It won't take him long to learn

After a nice sit and stay of about thirty seconds, off we go again. 'Fido heel', step out nicely for a few paces, then 'stop', 'stay', and repeat the process

There is no need to use a signal if the dog sits at your side, for the obvious reason that if you are walking along in the upright position and come to a normal halt, the signal cannot be seen! The verbal command should suffice

The forward leaning exaggerated 'stay' signal shown on the previous page is merely used in the beginning to steady the dog and build up confidence. However, having said that, signals are very important for distance control if you are considering going on to competitions at a later date. These will be taught in classes and each instructor will have his or her own ideas. (You may well have a few yourself of course.) The picture above right demonstrates the signal I use for medium distance control when I cannot use words on a film set

I have asked the puppy to stay and gradually worked my way around to the front and then by using the verbal commands which he already knows ('sit' and 'stay') and the signal simultaneously, he soon learns to combine the two. Later, of course, (much later) one can be clever and separate the instructions, sometimes using voice only, and sometimes using the signal alone. This is great practice! Don't try to be clever though. First things first as long as they associate their actions with the sit command. There are no hard and fast rules. I personally prefer it if the puppy is on his feet when he stops and stays, so I can demonstrate the *action* of the sit to him. Then he understands clearly that he is performing to order.

To teach a dog of any age to sit is very simple. A well-trained dog should, of course, sit wherever and whenever asked, but to begin one should choose the position most comfortable to oneself. If you want to get involved in obedience competitions in the future, then you must always ask the dog to sit at your left side. On the other hand, if you are simply seeking a well-behaved uncompetitive pet, then it is up to you. You may be left-handed or may just prefer the dog to sit on your right! This is fine! It is *your* dog and don't be browbeaten by 'experts' who tell you that the left-hand side is the *only* position. Either side is equally effective and, in fact, I always train from the front with the dog facing me – thus breaking all the 'rules'!

Always remember the dog is your property and you may educate it in any style you choose. Once a novice owner starts to worry about not conforming to the rules then the pleasure goes out of dog training. Our aim is to own a pet with immaculate manners, an animal to give pleasure both to ourselves and to others. It surely cannot matter how we achieve these ends, providing of course that we use only kind and humane methods. Training should be fun, both for the owner and for the dog.

For the sake of matching the photographs we will sit the puppy on the left-hand side. Simply hold the lead up in the air with the right hand and gently press his rear end into the sit position with the left one. Praise him in an even tone and ask him to stay. 'STAAAAAY.'

Reinforce his confidence if necessary by getting down to his level and stroking him, saying 'sit' several times to imprint the word and then praise but do *not* release him with a praise word. If you do, you may find in the future that every time you say 'good' your dog will think that the exercise is over and break. 'Good' spoken softly is a **reinforcement.** The words used should be entirely of your own choice – whatever you feel comfortable with. I simply use 'good' to let my dogs know that they are doing fine and then when the exercise is over I say 'O.K.'. This is the *release* and the permission to go bonkers and have a potty five minutes as a reward. *Then* loads of love and praise, but not until *after* the release word! 'O.K.' has a fine, sharp ring to it and I find it very suitable. However, say anything you wish as long as the relationship to the release is understood.

At this stage it is a good idea to keep mixing and matching the behaviours learned so far. This will develop his little brain at a rate of knots. Puppies are amazing creatures and will inhale learning like a vacuum cleaner. Likewise, of course, the puppies who are allowed to 'get away with murder' from the start absorb all the undesirable habits, from chewing to pulling, and it will be *these* behaviours which will become imprinted in their computers. These are often the poor creatures that end up in the dogs' home, or worse. Therefore, in order to prevent any bad or lazy habits developing we will just continue going over what he has learned so far, twice a day for short periods of, say, fifteen minutes.

Keep changing the order. Walk to heel then stay, then heel and turn and sit and stay, then heel and about turn, heel, sit and stay etc, etc; never forming a routine and always ending on a nice stay of a reasonable length and a release with loads of praise, maybe even a biscuit or a chew stick as a reward. Always take him indoors on a 'flyer'; quit on a good one before he loses interest.

One tip here is that if you are asking a dog to stay, it is important during the early stages that *you* are as steady as possible to give him confidence. He will pick up your vibrations and if you fidget or lose your concentration for just a second he may lose his also and break. Once properly trained, of course, he should remain steady with distractions, but this will take quite a bit of time.

Now will be as good a moment as any to make out your 'plan of campaign'. I always keep a training sheet, a record of my dog's progress and it's both fun and interesting to look back over the charts of several dogs of different types and ages and note the differences in development. It's often hard to remember just exactly what stage Fido was at a year ago. If you have a chart it's easy to check back.

Plan of campaign

The standards:

* ＊   Barely understands the commands.

* ＊＊   Has come along very nicely and will perform to order. This standard is most acceptable for the average well-behaved pet.

* ＊＊＊   The ultimate standard, where mistakes are hardly ever made. Steady and confident, even with distractions. Take as long as you like before granting ＊＊＊ (*years* if necessary).

In order for this system to work we must be scrupulously honest with ourselves. A ＊＊ dog is great! Good and steady, willing to please and obedient. Who could wish for more? It may well be that your 'student' has a favourite behaviour. One which he picks up in record time and *always* executes to perfection. Then just award him ＊＊＊ for *that* and ＊＊

NAME: FIDO.

BREED: TERRIER.

SEX: M.

AGE At Commencement of Training: 3½ MONTHS.	Use this space for any specific details of the dog's background, if he was rescued or had been badly treated for example				
HEEL	6th MARCH 1986 ✳	20th MAY 1986 ✳ ✳			
STAY	6th MARCH 1986 ✳	12th MAY 1986 ✳ ✳	30th JAN. 1987 ✳ ✳ ✳		
SIT	2ND APRIL 1986 ✳	16th APRIL 1986 ✳ ✳			
DOWN	3RD MAY 1986 ✳				
COME WHEN CALLED					
FETCH AND HOLD					

Example Chart, for any age after all vaccinations are completed.

*This shows that our 'student' took just over two months to grasp a good ** standard of the heel and stay behaviours and as he got into the swing of his training he took only just over two weeks to learn a good steady sit.*

By January of the following year his stay was superb!

for the rest. I recommend training classes to adopt this method too. It's a super way of keeping track of everyone and it makes awarding prizes on graduation day much fairer. Continuous assessment (recorded) is often very useful, particularly for comparing different breeds and their development.

Demonstration of a stay – definitely a ***! Pippin is steady and confident despite the distraction provided by Oliver

Reinforcing the stay

It's always a good idea to start reinforcing the 'stay' as soon as your little dog understands the first few basic rules. This can be done very easily by placing your student in the position which is most comfortable for him. The puppy in the photograph, Duffy, was trained to stay on his feet so he was happy in that situation. Sitting will do just as well. Don't worry. We are only aiming at making the stay more reliable. Place your puppy in a 'stay' position and stand next to him, showing the signal and giving the verbal reassurance. 'STAAAY. Good!' Now instead of the usual 'break' and on to the next behaviour, we will instead take one *slow and gentle* half step in front of him (see picture), repeating 'staay, that's good,

To reinforce the stay

Start from the 'stay' position, with a nice clear signal and lots of verbal encouragement, 'staay', etc

Take a half step ahead, remember the loose lead. Then take another half step round until you are facing your dog. If he fidgets and breaks, go back to the beginning and try again. Don't loose your calm, patient approach, just give him the chance to have another go

Moving slowly and steadily, take as many steps backwards as you dare without unsettling him, ideally to the end of your lead, still showing a clear signal and voicing encouragement. Wait about thirty seconds in the 'stay' position

Slowly and gently reverse the steps until you end up alongside him again. Wonderful practice this! Your dog may be sitting or standing. It really doesn't matter as long as he is comfortable

STAAAY'. Remain in this position for say thirty seconds then *gently* and *slowly* take one small step back until you are alongside again. Practise this slow manoeuvre several times at each training session until he is quite confident and happy to remain in one spot while you make your move. The success of this will all hinge upon your quiet confident and gentle approach. He will gain confidence from you, so don't at all costs move quickly.

He will soon get the message and after a week or so (don't rush it!) you may use the same method to take yet another half step round and several *slow and gentle* steps backwards until you end up facing him (see picture). The distance you dare take backwards will depend entirely upon the steadiness of your little dog (and *that* will depend entirely upon the steadiness of you!).

If you feel that he isn't quite ready for too much space between you, fine! Just keep on practising close work until he improves. As I have mentioned before, it doesn't matter how long he takes, just enjoy your training and he will too.

6

Behaviours and manners

Now we will try a bit of psychology. Let us assume that our little friend has got a good steady stay, and we are able to step back at least to the end of a six-foot lead. Stand and face him (see photo below) then slowly bend and lay the lead down on the ground (still maintaining your clear signal). Now in order to prevent him breaking too soon, you will have to be very careful not to excite him. As long as that lead is attached to his collar, he is still under control (or so he thinks!); quietly repeat 'staay good good', then after about thirty seconds drop down and 'O.K.' sharp and clear. Call him by name with *loads* of encouragement from a crouching position. He should run straight to you. He has no reason not to. You are pleasant

1 *Assuming your pet will stay at lead length, ask him to either stand or sit (whichever is the most comfortable for him) and 'staaay'. Keep your lead featherlight; have confidence and he will too*

2 *Gently lay the lead onto the ground and show a clear stay signal. Reassure with your voice 'staaay', 'that's good', etc. If you move quickly at the point of laying down the lead, you may unsettle your pet. Keep everything as steady as possible and maybe (if you have the courage) even take a few steps further backwards*

3 *When you feel that your little friend has 'stayed' for a reasonable length of time – thirty seconds (a minute maximum) – release 'O.K.', drop down and call in to you with loads of encouragement. (For the benefit of anyone who spots that I am wearing a jacket in this picture, it was taken at the same time as the others but the sun went in and suddenly it became very chilly)*

4 *'Here I am' – great! Mutual admiration all round. As your dog gets a grasp of the situation you can gradually extend the length of the 'stay'*

and inviting and *down at his level*! He will be beside himself with affection if you adopt the right attitude yourself. If you have something nice in your pocket, all to the good. If he has come straight to you, give him a little treat. He deserves it.

After a few seconds of mutual admiration, pick up the lead, regain your composure and steady him down. Start him off again from the stay position (either sitting or standing). Do a little bit of 'dressage', a few heels, sits, stays, etc in all directions, then stop again. Carefully and slowly back away and repeat the 'come when called'. It will prove absolutely invaluable in the future. This little exercise will be the basis of your 'come when called' behaviour (see page 65). Just mix and match as you continue your training. Sometimes asking your friend to stay until you return to him, and sometimes asking him to come to you. You *must* be the next best thing to hot dogs as far as he is concerned! You must *always* be a pleasant place to return to. Then when you call him he will have *no reason to refuse*. So if it takes a bit of bribery and corruption, so what? Many experts will say 'don't offer tit-bits' and you may well choose to refrain from using them later, once your association has been imprinted in his computer, but if it helps you to get started, why not? If you have to continue using the odd cookie, don't worry! It's your dog. You make the rules! He comes when you want him to and *that's* what matters!

Get down to it!

To teach a dog to lie down is not all that difficult. Adult males sometimes (not often!) have a tendency to resist being put into a submissive position, but this is easily overcome with a little time and patience. Once again, it's a case of trying to understand how an animal feels under a certain set of circumstances. If a male dog is on his feet, he is at his most powerful. Sitting is not too bad from his point of view, but unless he is relaxing, to ask him to lie down may make him feel vulnerable. The 'girls' and puppies do not seem to mind at all. So, how to go about it?

Just ask your dog to 'stay' in the sit position and depending upon which side he is at the time, take his front feet in your dominant hand and gently pull them forward, easing him down, at the same time applying a little gentle pressure with your other hand to his shoulders (see picture).

When his body is flat on the ground, keep on repeating 'Fido, *down, down*, staaay. That's good.' If he is steady enough, take just half a pace in front of him. Keep your own body low and show the 'stay' signal. After a few seconds of reassurance slowly return to his side (if possible without him making a move) and then after about another twenty seconds or so

Get down to it! Ask your dog to sit and stay. Then slowly walk around to the side and take his front legs in one hand, gently applying a little pressure to his back just above the shoulders with the other.

Pull the front legs forward and your dog should slide down to the floor in the flat position. Tell him to 'staaay down', repeat 'down' several times to help him associate this with the flat position.

release, drop down and praise. If you can manage to get him down at your first try, great! If not, don't worry, dogs like children are all different and some will, without doubt, take longer to learn than others. The main thing is that he understands what you want from him and can *associate* the word 'down' with the 'flat' position.

As you progress, you will be able, as in all of the other exercises, to step slowly round to the front of him and then eventually to the end of a loose lead. Once you are at this stage you are home and dry. I have always preferred a quiet gentle approach to new behaviours. They seem to register in the computer much more easily than trying to break any records with

If he seems steady, keep your body low and show the stay signal. Keep verbally reassuring and slowly take a step backwards.

Eventually you should be able to step back to the end of the lead and then stand up. Don't rush it, move slowly and try to make your wishes easy for him to understand

the 'quick march' method. What is more, these behaviours should be imprinted for *life* and it is important that they are taught in a fashion which will not build up any tension or resentment.

Once you have trained the down behaviour you will really have achieved a great deal. Congratulations! If you went no further, your dog should remain under control with the lessons learned so far. He will walk nicely to heel and he will stay when asked in either the 'sit' or 'down' position. This will mean that he will behave if out in a public place and will show a few manners and stay in his designated spot at home if non-doggie visitors arrive. How splendid! If you wish to go further and you have a taste for the 'big time' take him to classes at around six months of age. The fact that he has attended 'kindergarten' will put him streets ahead of other beginners. He will enjoy mixing with the dogs in a confined space; the experience will be invaluable.

If you feel that you would like to take your training a step further at home before, or even instead of, going to classes, try the extra long 'line of communication'. I have always found a line of lightweight, soft, fine rope to be the best for this purpose, at least twelve feet in length. Attach a small snap catch to one end and then off we go again.

Repeat all the behaviours learned so far, but with a greater distance between yourself and your little friend. The rope line will give you the opportunity to step *much* further away from your student. He will still remain in one spot if he sees the line and you should, in time, be able to ask him to stay in either the sit or down position and, holding the end of the line, walk *gently* round him in a circle of some twenty-four feet in diameter. This is quite an achievement. If you are successful give *yourself* a pat on the back after you have given one to your dog. Well done! Always remember, of course, that you will still ask your dog to walk close to heel with the line folded to a manageable length and then just play it out gently as you ask him to stay.

Eventually, try slowly laying the long line down on the ground, keeping your dog's attention at all times. After a few minutes 'stay', release, drop down and call him to you. This exercise will extend his area of responsibility and it will reinforce your 'come when called'. Wonderful practice indeed!

I won't spend much time on the heel free (off the lead) exercise because I don't believe it is really all that important for a pet dog. I cannot think of *one* good reason for a dog to be walking off the lead in the street and that really is the end of the subject! If your dog is loose in a safe play situation then it's the 'come when called' which you will need to practise, but the heel free is definitely required for advanced obedience competitions and this may be learned in classes.

Holly demonstrates the extra long 'line of communication'. Using a long line of fine soft rope, carry on practising the manoeuvres learned so far. The rope has a small snap catch at one end and this is used to make an easy slip collar. (Still check each time to be sure that it is put on correctly.) The slip is merely for gentle control and not for choking. This is evident in the photos. I usually start long line work with a rope of twelve feet in length and eventually advance to one of fifteen feet.

This type of training helps to instil confidence in the dog as the distance between you gets longer. After a few days of long line work, try gently (slowly does it!) laying the rope on the ground and asking your student to perform a few behaviours to order - 'sit', 'down', 'stay', etc. As long as he sees the line on the ground he should remain steady. The fact that it is attached to his neck will fool him into thinking that he is still under control and of course, he is, for should he break, stamp your foot on the end of the line and yell 'NO' (as his actions are undesirable) and then gently reassure him and try again. The shock will do him the world of good and no harm at all

You can try it out at home (off the streets of course) by asking the dog to walk to heel with the lead attached and then dropping it and letting him drag it along, keeping his attention at all times and constantly changing direction. Any corrections may be easily executed by just picking up the lead and 'checking' to keep him on his toes.

Eventually you should be able to remove the lead and attach a fine line, one which will fool the dog into thinking that he is free as a bird, but strong enough to catch him out if necessary (heavy duty fishing line attached to his collar is ideal). The ultimate is when you require no line of any description and this will only come with time and patience.

I still do not approve of anyone showing off on the streets. Walking a dog without a lead, in a public place, is very dangerous and, in many areas, against the law.

Fast and loose

Now we come back to the association of ideas! Remember your puppy is only a mere member of the canine species. He does not possess the superior intelligence of a human being and therefore if the 'come when called' exercise is to be performed successfully, you must remember he can only *associate*. For example, supposing he runs away and digs up the next-door neighbour's roses before your very eyes. (Great sport! His tail is wagging so hard it is almost falling off!) *If* it had been possible for you to have magically transported yourself into the middle of the rose bed to chastise him 'in the act' he would have associated his digging action with the 'no' command and his little brain would have grasped the fact that his actions were wrong. However, you cannot get to him in time to stop him, so eventually you manage to call him off and you scold him severely. RESULT: *utter confusion!* Why? Because when he comes back to *you* he gets a scolding, so he *associates* the action of *coming to you* with the reprimand. (The roses long since forgotten.)

So the lesson here is that coming back to you must always, and I repeat *always,* be associated with a pleasant experience. Despite the fact that you could willingly wring his neck for the actions he performed earlier, it is far better to give him lavish praise, and maybe even a treat, for returning willingly to you than to chastise him. Remember his limited intelligence compared to yours. Tackle the digging problem in another way – perhaps by baiting him back into the situation and hiding close at hand to admonish him 'in the act', so again he can *associate*. A short sharp spray with the hose would work wonders here from a hidden position, so as not to have the admonition associated with *you*. Drop the hose, then step out. Call him and soothe his wounded wet pride. He will soon learn that being close to *you* is far less hazardous!

Do not scold him when he comes back to you on any occasion. A strong 'come when called' could possibly avert an accident and maybe even save his life if he were to run out into the road in the face of oncoming traffic. The cardinal rule is *never* run after a lively puppy. This results in a chase situation which is great sport. If your puppy gallops off into the blue yonder, first and immediately yell 'no!' (because his action is against your wishes). Then shout 'Fido, come'. If he turns around to look at you (which he should) drop down into the crouching position and give *loads* of pleasant sounding encouragement. Stay down until he comes right up to you then lavish him with praise and maybe even give him a treat. By crouching down you do not seem so intimidating to the little fellow. A good strong 'come when called' can prove vital in so many situations that I cannot sufficiently emphasize the necessity to make it a pleasant experience.

Another alternative is to call him and run in the opposite direction for a little way and he will usually follow as he loses a little confidence in the situation when you leave him. Then drop down as he approaches and praise him as before.

Come when called

There is a vast difference between a 'come when called' and a 're-call'. They are *poles* apart, in fact I have actually seen 're-calls' performed on television in order to demonstrate to novice owners how to get their dogs to come back to them, when what the owners really needed was advice on getting their dogs to return when out for a run or in a play situation. What they were shown though, was a strictly controlled regimented re-call, performed in a polished robotic fashion.

Now, dogs are far from stupid! They know the difference between work and play and those particular dogs were under strict control and definitely *working*. They were superb but I felt like phoning the television station and saying, 'Please ask the trainer to release the dogs and send them off for a wild gallop and then demonstrate to the interviewer just how to get them back under *those* conditions,' because *this* was the help which was needed.

You will win no prizes crouching down and encouraging your dog to come to you, but if you are inviting enough you can bet your boots he will come bounding back with enthusiasm, and that's what counts. We are dealing with an animal mentality and, if we get back to basics, the way to any dog's heart is through his stomach. Many trainers will never use food as an inducement (or, at least they won't *admit* to doing so!). But I know for a fact that if a dog is out loose with the wide world to explore, you had better give him a darned good reason to come back! All the training in the world can go through the window if he sees a rabbit or another dog. A bit of chopped, cooked liver will usually work wonders when all the verbal inducements in the book have failed.

He may well perform his polished 're-call' to perfection in a controlled situation of course, with no tit-bits whatsoever. We are merely reinforcing his desire to return when free as a bird. As I've said, I only use food in the early stages of training and then 'once in a while' afterwards. This way, my dogs always return like rockets on the off chance that there may be something nice on offer! Plus, of course, as I mentioned earlier, they really have no reason to refuse as they have never had an unpleasant experience upon 'returning to base'. *Loads* of praise usually works wonders here!

Give a little whistle

Jiminy Cricket certainly had the right idea. A whistle can be invaluable to anyone who is not capable of shouting or is too self conscious to yell at their dog in order to get him to return to base. Particularly useful for older people, this method of calling a dog is a 'conditioned response'. But let's not get too technical! Just take it for what it's worth.

If you use a whistle, then you should use a small reward so that the dog will associate the sound with food.

How to go about it? Simple as long as you stick to the rules faithfully. Get a whistle and leave it on your kitchen work surface where you won't forget to use it. Now as you feed your dog his evening meal, blow just as you put the food down (just one sharp blast). The dog will probably give you a strange look and wonder what on earth you can be playing at. (Don't worry, everything will all come together in a few weeks!) Now each time you put food down, whistle at the *precise moment you lay the bowl on to the floor.*

After a week, or maybe ten days of this, leave your dog in another room. Don't make any sounds to indicate feeding time. Ideally, make up the food maybe half an hour earlier while your pet is out in the garden. Then when you are ready to feed, blow! I'll bet that your pet will dash from the other room in anticipation of a nice supper. As he comes up just give one more short, sharp whistle and lay down the food. Praise him and let him enjoy the meal. Continue calling your dog to supper by whistle for a month, never missing a single day! Don't make the mistake of trying to rush it. After a month the behaviour should be well imprinted in an older dog. Puppies catch on much quicker, but even so still continue at this stage for a full twenty-eight days before going any further along the line.

Now you can try something a little different. Take a pocketful of goodies into the garden; *tiny* non-fattening treats, no choc drops or lumps of biscuit unless you are prepared to take these calories into account at feeding time. Chopped, cooked liver is ideal, or bits of diced meat. Let your dog have a potter round then take out your whistle and blow. If he returns at once, feed him and praise. Then let him off to potter once more. After a few minutes repeat and continue to practise this exercise for a week or so in the garden before attempting to try it off the premises. In order for this method to work properly one *must* be prepared to whistle at meal times for the rest of the dog's life. It's easy really! It becomes a routine. It's quite a conversation piece with guests if you happen to feed your dog while they are around. If you feel a bit of a twit, wait until they have left. The extra few hours won't hurt your dog. He will be all the more eager to respond.

Eventually you should be able to get your dog to return from long distances, much further than your voice would carry, without straining your throat. If you start this method from the puppy stage it will work like a charm. You can always use a silent dog whistle if you prefer not to be too conspicuous. O.K. you purists who never use food as an inducement. It's the old story. Home base is the best place to be and the whistle and food will reinforce the situation. *Do* be careful not to over-do treats though. Please take them into account and don't over feed, for the dog's sake.

Keep up the good work

Now will be a good time to start to polish up the behaviours learned so far. Try asking your pet to sit in a corner of the kitchen and stay for a while. Perhaps you may be preparing the veggies or making a nice cup of tea (now that's a good idea). Keep on encouraging your pet to *stay*. Carry on your chores as normal, often turning your back on your dog and maybe even just stepping out of the room for a moment. A serving hatch works wonders here because if he fidgets you can reassure him through the window. Don't ask him to stay for long; a minute or so will do to start with, then either (the choice is yours) go quietly over and stand next to him and then after reinforcing the stay with words and signal, 'release' him. 'O.K.' Drop down to his level and allow him his 'freedom'. Show him how pleased you are. No food necessary here, or on almost any other occasion, with the exception of the *outdoor* free 'come when called'!

Then try the same behaviour again for a minute or so, but this time stand a distance away from him and keep him in the stay situation until you feel ready to drop down and 'O.K.', call *him* to *you*. This is wonderful practice for any dog. Never let him anticipate what you are going to ask him to do. Maybe take his cardboard box or basket into the kitchen and ask him to stay there for a while and then release him in either fashion by walking up to him or by calling him to you. This will develop his little brain in no time at all, without putting any pressure on him.

Until your dog is under control at meal times it's quite a good idea to pop him into his travel box or crate with maybe a chew stick or a nice big bone. This will help him to understand that he must NOT make a nuisance of himself. If he is happy and comfortable in the crate, this will do him no harm whatsoever.

As your little friend gets older you may ask him to 'stay' in various spots around the house for longer periods, until eventually as the months go by, he will remain happily in his cardboard box while the family enjoy dinner! This will really impress your friends, doggie and non-doggie alike! Always

Showing off! By now your little friend may well be steady enough for you to try walking round him

A good, steady 'stay' signal and off we go!

Use your less dominant hand (and that will depend of course upon which side the dog is standing) to hold the lead gently and with your other hand show the 'stay' signal. Move very slowly halfway round the back of your student. Talk to him all the time and whilst his head should follow you as he watches and listens, his body should remain still. (If it doesn't, don't worry, it will in time!) Remain in this position for about thirty seconds in order to keep him steady

remember to 'release' afterwards! Don't let *him* decide when it's time to come out! Eventually you will, of course, end up with the perfect 'pub' dog. Make no mistake about it! One who will wander into the bar with you and will settle under the table upon the word 'stay' and remain happily whilst you stroll up to order your pint. What could be better?

Manners most certainly 'maketh man's best friend'.

When you really feel that you have got your act together, you can show off a bit! Try *slowly* walking all round your dog (see also photograph

Move very gently round him until you are standing on his other side, still keeping your verbal encouragement going and showing a clear signal. After a few seconds move again round to the front and eventually back to the starting position

The hands in these photos show a featherlight hold on the 'line of communication'. This takes courage (it's rather like teaching a child to ride a bike and letting go!) but it really does help to instil confidence

If you ever get to the stage where you can step over him – well done! Quit for the day. Congratulations!

above). The hand signal and verbal communication is easily seen in the picture. Duffy is watching and listening to my constant chatter. 'Staaaay. That's good!' He is reassured. I must say, though, that walking all round a dog of any age is not easy as they have a natural tendency to turn with you. You just have to move as if you are treading on egg shells in order to keep your little friend steady.

Eventually it *will* happen. When you have got him up to the ✻✻✻ stage you will be able to jump over him! It will take a long time but is well worth the persistence. A perfect example of a ✳✳✳ stay is demonstrated by Pippin, with Oliver in full flight (see page 52).

If your student never reaches the ✳✳✳ stage, who cares? A ✳✳ dog is as solid and steady as any well-behaved dog ought to be. It doesn't matter a jot if he never graduates through K.9 university with a first-class honours degree! What *does* matter is that you have taken the trouble to train him conscientiously to a nice comfortable standard and that you are both happy with the situation.

Eye contact and praise

Eye contact is vital in good training. Some animal psychologists will say that eye contact means intimidation. I have always found to the contrary, that it establishes a bond. It helps to build up a strong relationship and what is more to the point, it maintains concentration! No dog will learn if he is gazing at the world around him and sniffing the flora and fauna. He will daydream and all your efforts will be wasted. Keep his attention at all costs, even if the rubbish you are uttering may well get you certified if overheard. Just jabber on until the time when you give him your next command, which should be clear and precise. He will soon learn the difference.

I have usually found praise to be extremely effective after an exercise performed well, but care must be taken not to 'wipe out' the last behaviour (erase from the computer) in your enthusiasm. We are aiming at imprinting and it is important that your dog goes indoors *remembering* what he has just learned. Sometimes a bit of reverse psychology is required. An adult dog (a wily old cuss) who may be resentful of training, possibly because of bad handling in the past, may view the process in an even poorer light if released and praised to the skies. His brain may see the praise as a welcome respite from the treadmill. Dogs who think this way should be treated in a different manner. After each training session keep everything low key so he will not be aware of any contrast. Just take him in after he has performed to order and let him quietly rest and think about it.

These dogs need their enthusiasm building and this is when a reward *can* work! Carry a pocketful of his favourite goodies and each time he performs *well* 'pay' him. When he doesn't, don't! Then when he goes back indoors he really *will* have something to think about! Once his confidence is restored you can gradually work round to the more conventional method of no food and using praise alone as a reward. A dog's mentality is different from ours. He doesn't speak the language or understand *why* he should be asked to perform actions which do not come naturally. *We* know what we are trying to achieve but he may not (at least in the beginning).

Toe the line

One of the saddest situations is when an elderly couple allow their devoted little darling to snap and yap at all and sundry. They will never correct it in public and probably never at home either. They will reassure the little creature with pats and kindly words, protecting their baby from the nasty people who dare to walk by with their dogs on leads. This will give their little horror more confidence to try harder. Love of animals can become so misguided sometimes that the end result could perhaps become dangerous.

What Fido *should* have in this case is a short, sharp clip across his rump the very *second* he voices his opinion, to enable him to *associate* his actions with the **NO** command and to understand that they are undesirable. Now, I'm *not* suggesting for one moment that one beats a dog in public, or anywhere else for that matter. All I am trying to say is that manners maketh man's best friend and a little sharp and instant correction administered in a fair but firm manner (tone of voice can work wonders here also) will go a long way to correcting the problem. Dogs who snap and yap are not to be tolerated. It takes courage to administer correction in a public place, and because of this many dogs know that they can get away with murder. Children who throw tantrums on supermarket floors are an embarrassment to their red-faced mothers. Some will take the bull by the horns and give little Johnny a severe dressing down in public, perhaps even removing him from the store until he behaves. Others just wish the floor would swallow them, and allow the child either to play out his tantrum or give in for the sake of peace and agree to the desired chocolate bar. Once this happens the child wins. He will most certainly try again. Children and dogs are similar in many ways. Look at the child and look at the parent. See the dog, see the owner.

A short, sharp, *instant* slap across a dog's rear end (just once), coupled with the sternest 'No' and verbal abuse, will do your pet more good than harm (and this is written by a genuine animal lover). Don't let him get away with bad manners. You will regret it if you do!

7

Diet and health care

'How much should I feed my dog?' What a question! I would much prefer people to ask 'How *little* should I feed my dog?' Quality is infinitely more important than quantity, particularly with puppies (we will get round to those a bit later). The fact is that man has domesticated the dog and is constantly trying to treat him like a human being, which he most certainly is not.

A waist of time

Back in the wild he would have had to track and hunt for his food and sometimes, when the pickings were slim, he could go twenty-four or maybe thirty-six hours before he made a kill. He would then gorge himself, sleep to rest and digest and then go off again in search of more sustenance. He would, without doubt, be lean, fit, mentally and physically alert! The strong survived and *thrived* on the lifestyle. The western world spends a *fortune* on its more pampered pooches, from luxury dog beds to toys, protective clothing for bad weather, expensive foods and so on. The market seems to get bigger every year. Great for the lucky dogs of course – they love it, but is it all that necessary? I still maintain a cardboard box makes a fine bed and can be thrown out and replaced for free. A happy, healthy dog doesn't need to luxuriate in a fur-fabric bed, and he doesn't need to gourmandize and pig himself in the kitchen either.

First assess your dog's lifestyle and be *scrupulously* honest! Does he live an active life? (What *he* would call active?) A full-time fit working dog requires considerably more food than a pet who spends ninety per cent of his life around the house with just a potter in the garden and a stroll in the evenings for exercise. When you say you take your dog for a walk twice a day, do you? (Now, be honest!) Do you actually walk a brisk outstepping stride from which you will both benefit or are you a member of the 'potter and pee' brigade? If these questions are honestly answered then the reply is your barometer. This is the way you will govern how much food your dog requires. Always, of course, check with your vet if in any doubt.

Your dog will probably be eating far more than he needs if he is losing his waistline and behaving in a sedentary fashion. I personally never feed an adult more than once a day. I use high-quality proprietary animal foods which are carefully researched to ensure that they contain all the nutrients required.

If my animals are working, I add a vitamin supplement or some protein in the shape of a cooked egg or fish. The older dogs are very carefully monitored and if they appear to be 'putting on a bit', I 'take off a bit' to balance and give them more exercise to get them back to their original weight. Likewise, if a bitch is spayed there is no reason whatsoever for her to get fat! Keep her fit by ball or stick play in the garden and lots of brisk walking and even if she appears hungry, don't give in! If you are certain that she is maintaining her figure on the amount fed, stop at that. Give her chew sticks or cooked marrow bones instead to keep her mind off food. Many spayed bitches become 'chow hounds' with insatiable appetites.

Common sense is always the rule. Biscuit meal is more fattening than lean meat or tinned food but is necessary in a balanced diet. It will supply roughage. The actual amount of meal will have to be decided upon by experimentation. There are some first-class tinned dog foods on the market, the majority of which require no vitamin supplement, but if you feel that you want to do the very best for your pet you can always add a *little* cod liver oil to his food each day and give pet multi-vitamins two or three times a week. Always read the instructions on the packet before administering and *never* overdose without consulting your vet. Cod-liver oil is great for the coat, but whether your dog will actually benefit from the additional vitamin supplement is open to question (providing, of course, that he is being fed a high-quality well-balanced food). Dogs never need vitamin C, in any case – they manufacture their own.

Never on Sundays

Shock! Horror! I only feed my dogs six days a week! I have *never fed an adult dog on a Sunday*. 'Oh my, how cruel!' I hear you cry. Yet my animals are all fit and healthy and extremely happy with the situation. Of course they would *like* me to feed them on Sundays, but I don't. I keep their minds off the subject by doing a bit of extra grooming and giving them something to chew. When I went to the States I was pleasantly surprised to find that the Frank Inn Organization, where I worked as a trainer, also never fed dogs or cats on Sundays (with the exception of puppies, kittens and invalids of course). Their animals were in the peak of condition. They had always to be looking their best in case they were called out to the studios. This method of feeding worked very well for them. I was relieved when I got there and found that I wasn't the only 'harsh' and 'cruel' crackpot in the world.

Now, I've always said, 'What's good for the dog is good for me – diet and exercise included.' I was chatting with a friend over coffee one morning and the subject of 'never on a Sunday' came up (her dog was looking just a *little* rotund at the time). Then after a bit of thought I put it to her that it wouldn't be such a bad idea if we tried it ourselves. Great! Which day was the next question. Mondays! As we are all (come on, be honest) fond of a good blow out at the weekend, Monday seemed like the best opportunity to give our systems a bit of a rest. (Not to mention the calorie count.) 'Let's call it "Mondays Off",' she suggested, and that's just what we did. So come on, join us in the 'Mondays Off' club. No fee. No diet required. No fad foods or chemicals. Just a nice rest for your poor old overworked digestive system. I drink either diluted fruit juice or lots of water on Mondays and never plan any visits to friends in the evenings, to ensure that I don't fall by the wayside. I start the day with a beaten egg in orange juice with a sprinkle of vitamin powder. Then nothing else except drinks until Tuesday. Great for the waistline and also for the conscience because as you serve your *dog's* dinner on Mondays, you can tell him that you are making the ultimate sacrifice in sympathy with him. Look the other way though, because I have heard it said that some dog foods are taste-tested by humans – I'm not averse to the odd nibble on a dog biscuit myself!

One final word on the subject. Many police and army dogs are only fed six days a week and they are living proof that the system works. Show me a fat police dog!

Puppies

Puppies are a whole different ball game. They require a nourishing, well-balanced diet with all the essential requirements for growth and development. Do not penny-pinch when feeding a puppy; give him the best you can afford. This doesn't mean that you need to produce a miniature blimp in the process. When I was young, and actually it's not that long ago (this century at least) my school friends had little brothers and sisters who were often entered in baby shows (they used to be all the rage). In those days it wasn't the prettiest, cutest, infant who won. No way! It was the moon-faced, overweight, Michelin-tyred and dimple-kneed . . . I could go on and on! Not so today, thank goodness. Doctors and dieticians have taught us the error of the ways of our parents. Fat babies make fat people, who in turn may suffer many side-effects such as heart or respiratory problems. So what's so different with puppies? They are notoriously greedy and unlike kittens, do not know how to regulate their food intake, so the responsibility lies with us.

Many breeders give diet sheets that are ridiculous, quoting pints of milk and cereals for breakfast, then lunch of meat and biscuits in vast quantities, then repeating again for tea and supper, etc. I met a girl just recently who only worked part time, but still had to ask for half an hour off each morning to rush home in order to give her four-and-a-half-month-old one of his *five* daily feeds! Her little dog was like a balloon. Grossly overweight and suffering from the 'trots'.

Think about it for a moment. What goes in must come out and the shorter time it has in the system, the less chance it has of doing any good. Now I'm not a qualified vet, but I do know what works for me. I find that to feed a high-quality balanced animal diet calculated according to the instructions on the can to ensure the *total daily requirement* of a puppy *according to size and weight*, divided into three meals with as *wide a space between them as possible*, works perfectly.

Example: Breakfast 7.30 a.m. Lunch 12.30 p.m. Supper, the lightest meal of the day (for obvious reasons) 6.30 p.m. This gives five hours between meals but still feeds the *total daily requirements*. If possible leave even wider spaces between by starting earlier (try not to feed after 6.30 p.m.). This method of feeding usually produces good, well-formed stools which are easy to pick up in the garden and proof of good digestion.

Now what about milk? 'Half a pint with Weetabix for breakfast', says one diet sheet. Quite honestly, if your dog never drank milk again throughout his entire life, after weaning, he would still remain fit and healthy, providing he has a good source of calcium and vitamins from the rest of his diet. Let's face it. In the wild, once an animal is weaned, it must go to the river to drink. No friendly milkman is going to drive into the forest to present him with two pints of gold top each morning! Many dogs and cats cannot assimilate cow's milk and this can be a major cause of diarrhoea in young puppies. In your efforts to do the best for your dog you are causing him problems by giving him what is basically an unnatural diet. Some puppies do well on goat's milk, but not all. If you really feel that you *must* serve milk because psychologically you feel that 'he's a baby and he needs it', give him the specially formulated imitation bitches' milk

Cow's milk v. imitation bitch's milk. I go for the powdered milk food every time, as it has been produced after many years of research. It is very easy to digest and ideal for young puppies, invalids and older dogs.

I still give water to drink under normal circumstances but if you feel that you must serve milk, then use the one which will be the closest to your dog's natural diet and you should have no problems with digestion

which is readily available in good pet stores - the milk powder used for infant puppy rearing. This should suit his digestive system, as it has been produced after many years of careful research. Or why not just give him a drink of water instead? And save yourself worry and expense.

If in doubt, ask your vet, particularly with regard to your puppy's correct weight-for-age ratio, and also for advice on feeding invalids.

Watch your step

It's not a bad idea to 'bother' a puppy (just a little bit) from time to time when it is eating. This will imprint into his little brain that if 'Pack Leader' (you) happens to wish to remove his bowl for a moment, then he must politely wait until it is returned.

There are many good reasons for a little gentle teasing when a puppy is either eating from his dish or chewing on a bone. A small child for example, maybe a visitor unused to animals, might toddle into the kitchen just as an adult dog was eating. Now if the child happened to stumble or fall onto the animal, the mind boggles at what might happen if the dog were unused to being interrupted. Likewise a blind or elderly person could accidentally kick the bowl with disastrous consequences.

Better to be safe than sorry. As your baby eats his meal, bend down and gently remove the bowl for about thirty seconds and tell him to 'stay', then let him have it back and reassure him with a little praise. Keep stroking him and maybe move the bowl around a bit. If he accepts this, then let him eat the remainder in peace. If he seems protective towards the food, either by putting his foot on it, growling, or both, then give a sharp tap on the nose and say 'No' (because his behaviour is undesirable) and then make him wait for a moment and let him eat some more. Try again and keep on trying until he learns a few manners. Please don't be cruel. Try to see it his way. His animal instincts will tell him to protect his food, but he will soon learn to toe the line if you are firm but fair.

One only needs to repeat this exercise about two or three times a week to start with and then just occasionally for the rest of his life after he understands clearly what is expected of him. As long as he *always gets the food back* within a reasonable length of time you should have no problems with his behaviour.

A dog's best friend

A good vet is worth his weight in gold! He should be the person you can go to with any problem, large or small; someone who will take a personal interest in your pet and treat it like his own. You need a vet that you can talk to with ease; one who will be available at any time to listen and to offer help, even when actual *treatment* may not be necessary. One who will give advice on ordinary day-to-day subjects, such as worms and fleas; kennel recommendation, diet and the like. One, above all, who has a high standard of hygiene. Vets like this *are* to be found but you have to search them out.

If you move into a new area or have just acquired your first pet, it is always a good idea to ask around locally and compare prices and services offered. Personal testimonials are usually the best, and I have always found both the post office and the pub to be fine sources of local information.

The post-mistress or the barmaid will probably be able to point you in the right direction.

The British tend to be uncritical in their choice of a vet, as with other things. My mother used to say that because she had lived through a war, she was conditioned into accepting, without question, anything that was dished out, after years of standing in queues and being grateful for whatever was on offer. The English hate to cause a fuss and will often walk away from an unsatisfactory situation rather than speak up, particularly where 'medical authority' is concerned. I know many people like this and I used to be one of them.

Why should we be inhibited about doctors and medical staff? Why, oh why, do so many people regard them with awe? They are just ordinary folk doing a job of work for which they have completed the required amount of training and satisfied some examining board that they are competent, in just the same way as your local civil engineer, solicitor, and plumber have done! Doctors and vets, of course, do deal with life and death and this sets them apart from the rest, but the point I am trying to make is that just because a person has a degree it doesn't mean that he is infallible and if you are not satisfied with any service you are getting from your vet, *tell him*! For heaven's sake, don't go home with that nagging doubt in your mind about some small point or symptom which you feel he may have overlooked. He is, after all, only human, and we all have 'off days'. Remember, you are paying for his services. Most professional people welcome clients who speak their minds. It really makes their job so much easier all round. They are then able to tackle the problems in a much more comprehensive way.

I doubt if I would have written these words had I not lived in the United States for almost seven years, where British inhibitions do not apply. My attitude has changed completely. No more will I place my unvaccinated, vulnerable puppy or kitten on to a table that is *dry* (possibly with a few hairs on it from the previous patient!). I need to see evidence that the table has been cleaned and disinfected, and even then I *always* spread out a towel before putting the little one down. The towel is then put into a bag and washed upon returning home. I don't return it to the carry basket – this would defeat the object. Paranoia, you may say. Common sense, I reply! Your baby animal is very precious and if you take it into an establishment which deals with all types of treatments and maladies, from the simple vaccination to highly infectious diseases, you should be as careful as possible.

Once your puppy is weaned he no longer has the in-built protection which nature provides in his mother's milk. He is at his most vulnerable until he has completed his first full course of vaccinations, so beware.

Don't be shy; simply walk in as I do and if the table is dry, just make some pleasant comment such as 'Sorry, have I come in a bit too soon?' Then, after the table has been disinfected, off you go. Quite simple. If they don't wipe the table, walk out. There is no national health service for pets and the choice is yours. You are paying good money to keep the person in business and if he doesn't come up to your expectations, find one who does.

I am extremely fortunate: I have an excellent vet and we have a fine relationship. He appreciates my point of view and respects it. No vet worth his salt will object to a client making some constructive criticism. It can only do good. In fact, how can he make changes if you don't tell him what kind of service you want? My vet opened a new surgery recently and actually held an open house and invited old and new clients to look over every vestige of the premises and make comments. What a splendid idea.

I shall be forever grateful to my good friend, Dr George Tuomy, from the San Fernando Pet Hospital in California. He opened my eyes to standards of hygiene far above anything I had been used to in Britain. Pristine protective clothing changed at *every surgery for himself and his staff*. The table sprayed with germicide between patients and wiped with disposable kitchen roll – thus avoiding even the slightest chance of spreading infection by using the same piece of sponge or cloth each time. 'Great, but all this costs money,' I hear the English vets cry. 'Rubbish,' I reply. What price the life of a precious pet compared to the cost of a few sets of drip-dry overalls, easily thrown into the washing machine in batches, and a year's supply of kitchen rolls!

The thought that some old-fashioned vets do *still* treat patients wearing the same old suit day in and day out (heaven only knows what they handle in a week) makes my hair stand on end. Thank goodness times are changing!

Travel sickness

One health care problem that can usually be dealt with *outside* the vet's surgery is travel sickness. It doesn't normally last over more than the first few trips in the car. Once again, the key is *association*. Make each trip a short and pleasant one and all should be well. If your puppy is too young to go out onto the streets due to lack of vaccinations, just pop him into the car and drive him around the block for five minutes or so each day, or take him shopping. He should ideally be in a travel box or cage, but if you don't have one, get someone to sit in the back seat with him to reassure him.

Once the puppy has had both injections, then a car trip to the park works wonders as this usually means the promise of a ball game or a nice walk at the end of the ride. The point is really that he won't get sick on short trips with happy expectations; just lengthen the rides a little at a time and *never* travel a puppy (or dog) on a full stomach. If you plan a long journey don't feed him *at all* on the day you travel until you get to your destination. Just offer tiny drinks at intervals and a nice meal on arrival.

I promise you that this is not cruel at all. It is far better that he is working up a good appetite on the journey than throwing his breakfast all over the car. If you are unlucky enough to have a highly strung dog who *hates* long journeys, you had better chat with your vet who will prescribe a mild sedative – something just strong enough to settle him down without knocking him out; still don't feed of course (common sense again!).

Given time, even hardened 'vomiters' can be won over, believe me. Eventually you may find that you can offer the sedative on the outward journey and not on the return. This is a major step in the right direction. Keeping a dog's attention often works wonders, so if someone can sit in the back of the car with him, it will be very beneficial. Man developed the car and is fully aware of its workings and advantages. A dog does not possess such knowledge. To him, it means motion and noise which may be unacceptable, at least in the beginning. He has no idea why he is being asked to spend time in this loud and smelly box on wheels and he may well be very frightened at first. Be patient and try to see it his way.

Keep an eye on your 'deposits'

Stools are one of the barometers of your pet's health and should be checked regularly. A healthy dog should produce nice moist well-formed stools of a good colour; although some dogs produce looser stools than others throughout their lives, and still remain fit and well.

Diet has a great deal to do with what is deposited. *Very* loose or watery stools can indicate over-feeding or unsuitable diet, but not always. *Tiny* quantities of bright red blood in stools may merely be the result of torn tissue (if they appear only once), but if copious or frequent, get down to the vet immediately. Dark blood usually means trouble and should be attended to as soon as possible. Likewise, nasty white, grey or 'jellified' stools *must* be dealt with professionally.

Dogs can, of course, like ourselves suffer from the odd 'upset tum' without any serious consequences and this can usually be remedied by a little Kaolin mixture and a chat on the 'phone with your vet.

Dry white chalky stools usually result from digesting bones and this, whilst not very desirable, isn't usually serious and will probably be remedied by the addition of a little cod liver or vegetable oil to the food.

Never take a chance. Check with your vet if you are in the slightest doubt over anything. *Any sudden change from the 'norm' should be investigated professionally.* Do go prepared though. Help your vet to do a proper diagnosis by telling him of any change of diet, environment or unusual situation which may have affected your pet. He will be grateful for your co-operation and your dog will benefit from the correct treatment. Your vet is only human and not psychic. If you don't tell him that your puppy devoured your vindaloo take-away last night, he may suspect something more serious.

8

Grooming

Regular grooming is necessary for the general health and wellbeing of your dog. I often ask people how they would feel if they went for weeks, or possibly months on end, without either combing or brushing their own hair (not to mention shampooing it). Of course they always say the idea is unthinkable! They would feel scratchy and uncomfortable within only a few days. So does your poor dog. He cannot speak and tell you that he would like a good brush down, but the sheer pleasure he shows in the operation usually tells you he enjoys it and feels a great deal better afterwards.

Top row:
Left to right. *(1) A soft bristle brush which will remove some loose hairs on smooth-coated dogs, but it is really more useful in imparting a nice healthy shine. Most dogs love the luxury of a good going over with a bristle brush. (2) An excellent tool for 'getting to the root of the matter'. This multi-bladed, matt-splitting comb will be of tremendous help when grooming out dogs with thick tangled coats. Use it carefully; the blades are sharp but are very well designed with blunt ends (not easily seen in the picture) to ensure that your pet will be safe. Even so, use common sense when grooming any dog with a sharp tool. There are instructions on the box. The comb is manufactured by 'Oster'. (3) A wire grooming mitt, wonderful for a brisk going over on a short coat. Helps to keep dogs free of loose hairs and the massaging action will get the old circulation going at the same time. (4) A steel comb with teeth in two sizes. A good all-round tool for any dog*

Second row:
Left to right. *(1) Rubber groomer for smooth coats. It will massage and help to remove sweat and dirt. (2) Flea comb, essential. The fine teeth will draw the eggs and flea dirt to the surface of the coat. Not easy to use on long coats (if tangled) but well worth having. Remember though that if your dog's coat is matted, it would be very painful to try to comb him through with teeth so fine. So it is the old story, keep him well groomed and it will be easy*

Bottom row:
Left to right. *(1) Three different types of nail clippers – all good. My advice to the novice would be to take your dog to a good groomer to have his nails clipped professionally, and ask her which type of clipper she would recommend for your particular breed. The only advantage with the clipper on the far left is that it has replaceable blades. There is also a tub of 'Clip Stop' in the picture. This* must *be purchased with your clippers and* never *attempt to cut nails without it. The instructions are on the container. The powder will stop bleeding in a matter of minutes if packed into the tip of the problem nail (see page 87). (2). Two excellent 'rakes'. The big one is ideal for large dogs – Shepherds, St Bernards and the like. The smaller version is good for any size (long or shaggy-coated) dog if you wish to remove dead undercoat. Please be careful though; don't yank out painful lumps of hair. Keep your pet in good shape by regular grooming and then a good rake out, to get rid of the worst hair during the moulting season, will be no problem. (3) The good old slicker brush, shown here in two sizes. One of my favourite tools. Great to use when drying a glamorous breed as it separates every hair as you 'blow along' (see chapter 9). This gives a wonderful finish to any coat but especially to the long and silky types. This brush is also excellent for everyday grooming and can be bought in many sizes. One small enough to carry in the pocket would be fine to use when out for a walk in the woods*

There are some people who actually think that grooming is cruel. These are usually folk who see show dogs on TV put through hours of rigorous ablutions in order to enhance their chances of making the 'big time'. I must confess that even I don't like to see good working animals 'prissed and ponced' with bald legs and pom poms. However, having said that, I am a firm believer in keeping a high standard of hygiene with regard to dogs that live in the house, for our mutual benefit.

Any vet will tell you that a glossy, tangle-free coat with no parasites will go a long way to enhancing your pet's general health and wellbeing. Some of the longer-haired breeds look lovely with simple all-over clips which won't win prizes in the show ring but will save hours in grooming time and housework. The Old English is one which immediately comes to mind. Many pedigree toy dogs with very long coats look sweet with a nice trim to keep the sweeping hair out of the dirt

Now fully grown, Duffy demonstrates the before and after looks.

What a door mat! It is most important to gently remove all the matts and tangles before shampooing a long-haired dog. This may take time, but is well worth the effort. Even smooth-coated dogs should be brushed right out to loosen hair and debris before going into the tub

What a swell! Only a mongrel but he would surely pass for one of his posh pedigree cousins. The hair has been carefully trimmed to reveal a pair of gorgeous eyes. (I'll bet he's glad that he can see where he is going at last!)

The coat nicely groomed and free from tangles should be easy to maintain from now on, providing a few minutes are set aside each day for a brush and comb out. Only common sense really, as the little dog must surely feel better for his 'make over'. A clean, sweet-smelling pet is so much nicer to live with. Fleas love dirt and you can't tell me that he's not happier feeling smart and sassy.

Compare the two pictures and judge for yourself

Most dogs can be trained from an early age to *associate* grooming with a pleasurable experience and with the shorthaired breeds it is relatively easy. A simple comb-through each day with a flat wire groomer to loosen dead hair should be followed by a good going over with a bristle brush in the opposite direction to the hair growth, removing loose dirt particles, and then again in the right direction for a nice smooth finish, followed by a wipe over with either a piece of pure silk or a damp chamois to impart a healthy gloss, and that is all. If done daily it should only take about ten minutes and your dog will thank you for it.

With the long-haired or shaggy breeds it is not only desirable but *essential*. To leave a long-coated dog ungroomed is downright cruelty. The hair becomes dirty and matted, harbouring bacteria and parasites. The dog scratches because he ·is uncomfortable and red patches appear. The end result is misery. I have seen dogs belonging to well-meaning people brought in for grooming, so badly matted that their collars have had to be cut away. One of the most infuriating things a groomer has to face is the owner who insists that the matted hair be combed out and not cut away to avoid 'spoiling the dog's appearance', preferring to put the poor little fellow through absolute agony having the hair balls yanked out.

A good conscientious groomer faced with this problem will either refuse to tackle the job and recommend stripping as the only solution or she will take her time over the dog, preferring not to put him through too much torture at once. It causes painful red 'hot spots' where the fur is pulled, so she will rest the poor creature between sessions, and possibly keep him overnight, maybe even another day. The end cost for the service will be astronomical because of the time and skill involved. If you don't mind my saying so, you will get what you deserve if you allow your dog to get into such a state. I have no patience with you.

Professional grooming establishments

Many people imagine that these deal exclusively with pedigree dogs and that they are purely for pampered pooches with personality problems. Nonsense of course! They are good, basic wash-houses for any type, any breed, any size or shape. They provide an excellent service if you don't feel like tackling the job yourself.

Anyone with a back problem, for example, should never attempt to lift a dog in and out of the tub, particularly if it is of a larger-than-average type. Far better to pay out a few extra pounds and have the job done by the pros. How nice it feels to call into the salon to collect your dog and be greeted by a happy, clean, sweet-smelling pet instead of the stinky, dirty creature you left there a few hours earlier. Well worth it I can assure you.

Trimming claws

Check your dog's claws from time to time, particularly if he doesn't get much exercise on hard ground. The quick is easy to see in white nails but it doesn't show so well on black ones. If you feel a little apprehensive about trimming your own dog's nails take him either to your vet or a good groomer.

If you decide to tackle the nails yourself (assuming that you have bought the correct clippers for the job), be careful not to catch the quick as it will bleed. If you *do* it isn't as painful as it looks and can be stopped by applying a little 'clip stop' wound dressing powder, which you should purchase from the dealer at the time you buy your clippers (just in case). Should you cause a nail to bleed, don't panic, just apply the powder by 'packing' it into the tip of the nail with your finger and then put the dog somewhere where he can stay quietly in one place until the bleeding stops. You should of course have sat him on a towel during the operation (newspaper is o.k. but it tends to be a bit slippery). Take him and the towel to a place where he can't paddle around all over your carpets. The warmly recommended travel box or case is ideal, but if you don't have one, carry the dog to a place with a washable surface like the bathroom or tie him up for a few minutes on a short lead, on his towel, in a safe spot in the garden. Use a leather collar – NEVER restrain a dog using a choke chain if he is to be left!

The nail will usually stop bleeding in a matter of minutes and I promise you that your dog will survive the ordeal with no problems. Many a vet has had a smile when some griefstricken owner has rushed into the surgery with a pet sporting a bleeding nail, only to find that it stops almost before they have had a chance to explain how it happened. Of course, there is *always* the exception and if your dog happens to pull back just at the crucial moment and the claw gets severely damaged, then of course it should receive treatment at once, but just nipping the quick slightly looks much more serious than it really is.

If in doubt, have the treatment done by a professional and then in future try to give your dog regular road work to keep the nails in trim. Older and obese dogs tend to get long nails due to lack of exercise, so get out and about a bit more – it will do you both some good! Always finish a clipping job with a small, flat, file giving a few strong strokes in a downward direction to remove any rough or sharp edges (lethal on tights). A young puppy's needle-fine claws will soon wear down with a little *regular* light road walking, but watch them as he grows older.

Speaking of claws, I must mention the hind dew claws. These are actually on an extra digit, or 'thumb', slightly higher up on the legs on the inside. On most breeds these have been eliminated over several generations but the odd ones do still appear. In the event that puppies are born with hind dew claws, the breeder should arrange to have them removed at about five days after birth. If by chance you *do* purchase a dog or puppy with hind dew claws still present, have them removed by a vet immediately. They are undesirable and have been known to grow into large, unsightly 'hooks' which have a tendency to get caught easily and can rip the inside leg severely. Only the *hind* dew claws are taken out, not the front ones.

Ears

Check your puppy's ears regularly for dirt or wax. Clean them gently with a cotton ball or a Q-tip soaked in a proprietary ear cleaning solution from either your pet shop or vet, then wipe them dry with a clean cotton bud or Q-tip. *Never* use the same cotton for both ears, to avoid cross-infection, and do *not* poke down the ear canal; Q-tip manufacturers warn that this is very dangerous. If you notice any discharge or inflammation in the ears, check with your vet. Mites can cause discomfort and can be easily treated if caught in time.

A knotty problem

Knots and nits go together like, in the words of the song, 'love and marriage'. It is a vicious circle. One leads to the other. Even relatively smooth dogs get matts and tangles if they have longish hair around the backs of the ears or feathering around the legs and feet, and long- or silky-haired breeds need constant brushing and combing to keep on top of the problem.

Matts and tangles are caused by loose hair being combed or pushed into balls by the action of the dog scratching. This will account for those nasty lumps which appear behind the ears. Now each day as the dog scratches, more loose hair is packed into the matt with the nails. This doesn't necessarily mean that your dog has fleas (at least, not at first). There are many reasons for a dog to scratch. An ill-fitting collar often creates the situation, as can ear-cleaning or a new shampoo. But in any case, if the loose hair *is brushed out daily, the matts cannot form*. If they are left, then look out chaps! Here come the nits!

Fleas are the original squatters and *love* a nice warm knotty place to hide, so they move in. This creates more scratching, which in turn creates bigger and better hair balls. Oh dear! Here we go – knots and nits. The solution is so simple. Five or ten minutes a day, preferably outside with a good steel comb and a slicker brush, would prevent all the problems. If hair balls become too big the only solution is either to cut them out yourself or go to the groomer and have them removed with a professional matt splitter. If you cut them out yourself you run the risk of spoiling the appearance of the coat until the hair grows again. A groomer can, as I mentioned earlier, remove matts professionally but the process is time-consuming and costly. Sometimes the only solution (providing the weather is warm) is a clean sweep by having your dog's coat stripped or trimmed down to a reasonably manageable length. This gives you a nice new start and, hopefully, in the future you will be able to keep control of the situation.

If you rescue a dog from an animal shelter it is advisable, as I have already suggested, to have it checked over by a good groomer *before* it ever enters your home. In my shop in the States we offered a service to anyone rescuing a dog, whereby if they called in on the way back from the pound (or dogs' home) and had the animal shampooed, we gave a free flea and tick dip, manicure and strip if necessary. This was our way of saying 'thank you' to the folk who were kind-hearted enough to give the dog a home and we made many new friends and long-lasting customers at the same time.

I would never advise anyone to take a dog straight into the house from the pound. If you decide upon rescuing an animal, make an appointment with your groomers. Drop the poor creature off on the way home and ask the parlour to give him 'the works'. You can then be sure that he won't carry dirt or parasites into your home and pass them on to any other family pets you may have. Makes sense!

Parasites

If you discover fleas on your pet (dog or cat) check him for tapeworm as well, as they often cohabit. Similarly, if you notice the signs of tapeworms, such as small white rice-like segments around the anus, then treat for fleas also. The two go hand in hand. *Always* consult your vet if in doubt, but both should usually be tackled at the same time. Tapeworm segments get into the dog's bedding without being easily detected by the human eye.

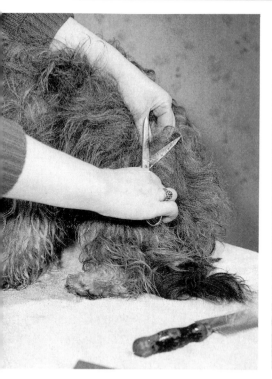 

Left: Wrong! By chopping a chunk out of the hair crosswise, you will leave the dog with an ugly step in the coat which will take a long time to grow again. If this is done all over the body, the poor creature will look awful! If you don't feel confident enough to split the matts yourself, take your pet to a good groomer who will either do the job for you or recommend a 'strip' or all over 'short back and sides'. (This should only be done in warm weather of course.) As the hair grows in again, keep on top of the situation with regular grooming. Prevention is always better than a cure.

Right: Correct! Carefully split the matts or tangles from roots to tips, guarding the sensitive skin area with your other hand. If you feel you haven't got the confidence to tackle the job yourself, take your pet to the pros. It is not that difficult actually, if you take your time (days if necessary)

The flea larvae which are developing from eggs laid on the warm blankets will eat the segments. Then as they grow into adults they will jump back onto the dog's body to feed from its blood.

The dog will undoubtedly ingest some of the fleas as it bites at its fur to quell the itch (or licks itself for any reason). The tapeworms will then redevelop in the dog's gut eventually to expel themselves once more in segments into the bedding. A vicious circle indeed and a *very* strong case

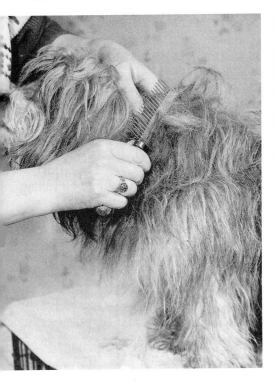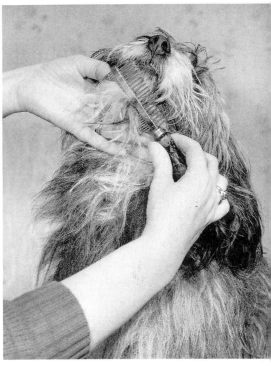

Left: As painlessly as possible gently tease out the split matt. This will leave the hair a bit thin at this point, but it will look much more acceptable than a bald patch which would result from cutting crosswise

Right: Saliva matts. Nasty knots frequently arise from saliva and food debris clogging up the hair around the mouth. These must be gently teased out with a comb and split if necessary with scissors, being very careful to cut from the root to the tip of the matt and not chopping a 'chunk' out which will ruin the appearance until the hair grows again. Guard the skin area with your fingers to ensure that you don't have an accident. If your dog isn't steady enlist the help of a friend to hold him. Keep him well combed out in the future; this will make life easier for everyone

for constantly changing bedding and keeping the dog's sleeping quarters regularly deinfested. If one gets to grips with the situation from the start, it's easy. Parasites have a debilitating effect on any animal, so it's in the dog's interest and *yours* (particularly if you have small children who don't wash their hands too often) to keep the problem in check.

Regular treatment for roundworm is also a good thing. Tablets are readily available in pet stores. Just follow the instructions for size and weight and repeat as directed on the box.

Before any dog is shampooed he should be completely free from matts and tangles. This makes it easier both to bathe and dry him. Comb and brush him out in sections, working your way all over the body a bit at a time. You may not necessarily do him all over in one session. If his coat has been neglected it may take you several days to ensure that he is completely tangle free, but it is well worth the effort. Take care to remove the matts and tangles gently by teasing them out with a comb or slicker brush. If they are very bad it is better to remove them altogether. If you decide to cut them out, try not to chop chunks out of his fur or you will spoil his appearance. This causes ugly steps in the hair which take several months to grow out. Gently split the tangle by cutting through it lengthways with sharp, small, scissors (ideally with rounded ends) as in the photograph on page 90 (*right*).

Be very gentle and always guard the root area by the skin with your hand to avoid accidents. When the matt is split it should be relatively easy to gently 'tease' it out with a broad-toothed steel comb. If this process is used all over the dog's body it will most definitely thin the hair, but it won't have that nasty 'chopped' appearance, which is the result of just cutting out the tangles crosswise. It takes much longer this way but it is a far more professional method. Ideally, of course, the situation should not arise in the first place!

Short-coated dog, eh?! This picture demonstrates what lies beneath the surface. Twice a year German Shepherds shed like sheep. But don't be put off this noble breed by the photo – just groom regularly and you should have no problems

Many dogs like to lie down to be groomed. This is quite all right if you have no objections. I always believe that if a dog is comfortable it doesn't really matter, so long as I can get on with the job relatively easily. My old German Shepherd loves to lie on his side when he is being brushed and combed and quite audibly grunts with pleasure throughout the process. German Shepherd Dogs shed like old stuffed mattresses twice a year! We left my old Max without grooming for three weeks especially for the picture, just to show the incredible amount of wool which comes out. I explained to him that he was being 'neglected' in a good cause to allow us to demonstrate to would-be Shepherd owners just how much work is involved to keep what appears to be a relatively short-haired dog in good condition. These dogs require raking out regularly and wire brushing daily, *especially* if they live indoors. The amount of undercoat which they shed is amazing. Max tried to understand, but was *most* relieved when he was taken down to the woods and finally groomed out again.

Strictly for the birds

Creatures in the wild all help each other in the ecological cycle. Birds will line their nests with wool left on the hawthorn hedges as the sheep rub by. We can also do our bit for the environment and save ourselves a load of housework into the bargain. I *always* take a wire brush and comb with me whenever we go out walking. This has become a routine over the years. Everyone has a quick going over before either jumping back into the van or just strolling home on the lead and the combings are left somewhere where they won't look untidy, usually stuffed under a bush in the woods or in the hedgerow. The birds take most of the hair in record time and the rest is all biodegradable natural wastage.

My old boss in the States, Frank Inn, used to say you can always tell a good professional trainer – someone who is *never* without a comb. I must say that since working for him I never go anywhere with a dog unless I carry at least a small pocket-sized comb, and use it whenever I get the opportunity.

9

Soap opera

Question: How often should I shampoo my dog?
Answer: Whenever he needs it!

A well-groomed, sweet-smelling dog is a pleasure to own and if you value your carpets and furniture it will be in both your interests (his and yours) to keep him in good condition. Many of the tough working breeds go for months or even years without a proper shampoo. Some farm dogs living outdoors may go their whole lives without ever having a bath. I used to know an old man who swam his dog in the river regularly and swore that it was in perfect condition. I suppose one might argue that in the wild this would be the only way any animal could clean and refresh itself. However, man has domesticated the dog and invited him in to share his home and lifestyle. Therefore, it is not unreasonable to expect that in return for the luxury of living indoors with all the creature comforts on offer, the dog succumbs to being kept in a clean and hygienic condition. It's not too much to ask! So, how to go about it yourself?

Have you got a strong sense of humour? Number one asset if you want to have a go at shampooing your dog at home. If you don't, then rush straight to the yellow pages and let your fingers do the walking over the Gs, for Groomers! Most professional groomers are first class. All the girls I have ever known in the trade (and a few boys too!) have been genuine animal-lovers – the main reason for their entering the profession in the first place. They are usually caring and sympathetic. If in doubt, your vet should be able to recommend a good parlour. Some vets, not many regretfully, do actually offer the service themselves if they are not too busy. They will most certainly help with ear cleaning and nail clipping if you don't want to tackle the job yourself. It all depends upon the size and breed of the dog and how soon you start to get him used to being bathed. The absolute ideal is from a puppy.

A shampoo need not be a traumatic experience for *any* dog if it is approached correctly, and puppies accept it as part of their lifestyle if they are introduced to it in a kind and intelligent fashion from the start. I know many people will read this and put up their hands in horror at the thought of shampooing a puppy. Why not? You bathe a baby, so why not a puppy? It is the ideal time to get him used to a situation which will recur for the rest of his life. Whether he needs it or not, a gentle introduction to a shampoo at about 3–4 months is ideal training for your little dog. Use a mild baby or puppy shampoo and have some eye lotion ready, some cotton wool or Q-tips, lots of warm dry towels, a hair dryer with a gentle setting, a brush and comb, and some conditioner if the hair is long.

Are we sitting comfortably? I'll bet we're not! Then we'll begin. Oops! Hang on a minute. Are you dressed for the occasion? You probably think that a nice plastic apron is fine. Of course it is if you have webbed feet! If your dog shakes, you will get the lot and it will just run all over the floor. Use an old thick towel tied around your middle. Very stylish if the milkman just happens to ring at the crucial moment! But much more practical and absorbent. I hope I'm not putting you off. Actually, shampooing your own dog is fun and economical too, and given a little experience on both your parts as the months go by, you will become very fast and proficient and a sparkling clean dog is *so* much nicer to live with.

First, either fill the wash basin or a large bowl or bucket with elbow warm water; just the same temperature as a baby's bath, a gentle heat. Then run about four or five inches of water into the bath tub at a similar temperature. Now let us assume that by four months old your puppy understands the two words 'stay' and 'no'. These should suffice to control him under the circumstances. Pick him up and gently stand him in the bath. Stroke him and reassure him verbally and tell him to *stay*. He may well try to climb out, but this is where he learns that he cannot go through life having everything his own way. Just hold him firmly and gently in the bath and repeat 'stay, good dog, that's good'.

Some dogs like to stand with their front feet up on something like a soap tray for steadiness and security. This is fine actually, as it helps to keep all the water running downwards out of the eyes. As long as he *stays* and he is comfortable, this is quite all right. Now take something suitable to use for ladling, a small saucepan or a plastic jug for example, and soak him all over with the bath water. Try your best to hold his head up and pour the water from the top of his head backwards to avoid the eyes. If you own a long-haired breed like a Shih Tzu or Lhasa Apso, then it is important to wash all the facial area but if your puppy is relatively smooth around the head you may prefer not to wash this part (at least for the first time).

Now apply the shampoo according to the instructions on the bottle and work up a nice lather with your fingers. Talk to him *constantly*, telling him he is good and to *stay*. If you keep a firm hand on him he won't shake. If you relax, beware, you will end up as wet as he! Take extra care if you are using either a medicated or flea shampoo. These can really irritate the eyes. And here's a good tip – shampoo is a lot easier to apply if slightly diluted and decanted into an empty washing-up liquid container. Much less wasteful as it can be much more accurately applied.

After you have given him a good soaping, release the plug in the bath and then gently rinse him with the clean water from either the basin or bucket which you have standing by. It must surely go without saying that one doesn't rinse with the same water one has lathered with, but I will say it just in case. It is only common sense to keep running nice fresh *clean* water through the fur until every drop of shampoo is gone, taking extra care to rinse the genital areas well – this rule applies equally to male and female. Some dogs can be allergic to certain shampoos on their most sensitive parts and they can become very irritated if not rinsed properly.

After your dog has been thoroughly rinsed, mix up a small quantity of conditioner at half strength and pour this through the hair. Rinse once more lightly and then holding him firmly by the shoulders to prevent him from shaking, wrap him up in a nice warm towel. If he has hairy feet, wring them out. Sounds funny, but just squeeze out all the surplus water by hand to save time on drying. Then if he is small enough, lift him up onto a chair or table at a comfortable height and rub him as dry as you can with the towel. The more water you can get out at this stage, the quicker he will dry. Then clean out both ears gently with either cotton wool balls or Q-tips (remembering to use these correctly, not poking them down the ear canal or using the same piece for both ears).

Wash eyes out after shampooing with any good proprietary human eye wash. Optrex is good or Artificial Tears. I have this on the good authority of my vet! Beware though. *Never* use a stale solution from the back of the medicine chest. This will do more harm than good. This rule applies to all medications (animal or human). Never keep any pharmaceutical products longer than a month to six weeks or, to be on the safe side, check the expiry date on the bottle or packet (if there is one!).

A load of hot air

Now to dry him. There are various methods, all quite suitable depending upon the breed, coat texture and time of year. If you have a smooth or short wire-coated dog he will dry very quickly with a hair dryer on the

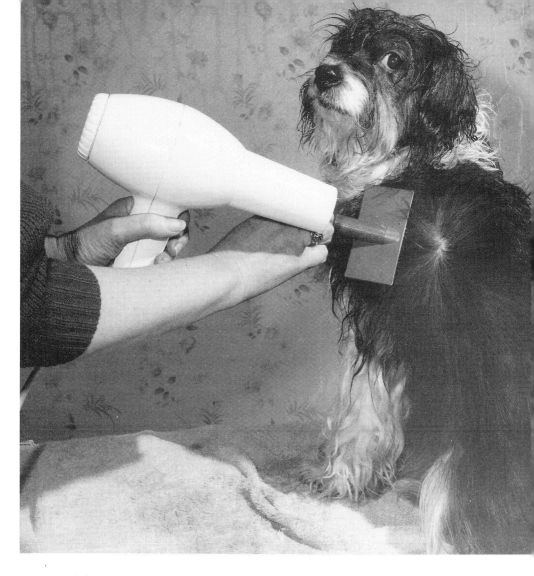

Pippin models the 'Wet Look'

Hand drying. Having first tried out the dryer on one of the most sensitive parts of your arm (between the wrist and elbow on the under side), go ahead and start to brush and dry your dog, working along each area a bit at a time. Keep brushing as you blow. This separates the hair and allows it to dry faster. Also the brushing action deflects the heat from the dog's skin where the hair parts to a 'rosette' as shown in the picture. It will dry from the roots outwards and the brush will remove the odd tangle which may have got through the net on the initial dry comb out.

If your dog is inclined to move around a bit, ask the help of a friend who can hold and reassure your pet, leaving you with two free hands to go ahead with the drying process. You may rest your dog of course between 'goes' but not for long as he must not catch a chill. Wrap him in a warm towel if you stop. Any dog hand dried in this fashion will look very professional and 'glam' indeed! The perfect time to try your hand at a bit of 'choc box' photography! (See 'after' photo of Duffy, page 85) warm setting. If you get someone to hold him and reassure him it will take no time at all to give him a good blow over and a groom with a slicker or bristle brush to remove the final few loose hairs.

Some dogs are scared of hair dryers but they can be made to learn that the process is harmless and, in fact, many dogs grow to really enjoy it. They love the feeling of the gentle warm air, not to mention the attention! If you own a neurotic dog, well, that is different, but if you have a normal, healthy, smart little critter, don't allow him to make up his own rules. *You* know that what you are doing won't hurt him in any way so you must kindly but firmly convince him likewise. The obvious proviso is that you don't train a hair dryer on a warm setting on *one spot continuously* – try it on your own head: it burns!

It is really a splendid idea to introduce a young dog to a bath at your earliest opportunity to avoid resentment in later life. Young puppies usually accept it very well, even if they are a bit lively.

If your dog has long silky hair then you will need the help of a second person to gently hold and reassure whilst you dry him. I say this because you will require both hands for the operation. Hold a wire brush in your dominant hand and your dryer in the other one. Now aim the jet of air at the fur until it parts to the skin and forms a 'rosette' (see picture). Now, as you blow, so you brush, slicking the hair from the skin to the tip. Keep brushing as you blow, making absolutely sure that the dryer isn't too hot. Test from time to time on a sensitive part of your arm. Your hands are far too tough to be accurate. As long as you keep the brush moving you will deflect the heat and the dog will not become uncomfortable. You will be surprised how much loose hair you will remove this way and the conditioner will have made the job so much easier.

Keep stopping to clean the brush out with a comb, to ensure efficiency. If the wires become clogged with hair they cannot dig as deep. Despite the word 'dig', beware not to be too rough or you will cause what we call 'brush burns' i.e. red areas from over-enthusiasm.

If you have done your homework correctly and your little dog (or big dog) was free from tangles at the start, then you can even *comb* out the loose hairs as you blow. But there can be no doubt about it, for a truly professional finish you can't beat a blow dry and a slicker brush – ask the pros.

Keep moving along from area to area until your dog is dry all over, brushing and blowing in all directions. Small silky dogs like Pekes or Lhasas look superb after this treatment. Blowing and brushing against the hair growth gives them body and fullness, making them look very 'glam' indeed. Most of the little show-offs seem to know it too. They love to feel clean and fresh and will parade like peacocks when it is all over. Larger breeds, such as Afghans, look gorgeous after hand drying, but they can be 'cage dried' or even SUN dried if the weather is kind, with quite good results; more than adequate for a pet who doesn't go to the shows.

Cage drying

If you cage dry you will (of course) need a cage or travel box large enough to allow the dog some room to stretch out and turn around. Let us assume that your dog is used to his box and is quite happy to sit inside on a nice

Cage drying. The dryer is set at a nice comfortable heat well back from the cage, propped up on towels at a suitable height. The cage is standing on the towel to ensure that the dog doesn't dig it up and drip onto the floor. Cover the cage with another towel to trap the warmth but leave space for a free flow of air.

An almost identical set-up may be used for 'sun-drying' outdoors, using the top towels to give shade. Always secure shade towels with either clothes pegs or weights to ensure that they do not blow away.

Never leave a dog alone in a drying situation, just in case.

If you dry your dog in either of these ways, it is essential that he is brushed out completely from roots to tips afterwards. This should be relatively easy if you have done your homework correctly and removed all the matts and tangles before he was shampooed. Conditioner helps to make the job easier, of course

pile of towels whilst he dries off. Place the dryer on the lowest setting, some distance away from the box, aimed through the bars at the front and propped up, if necessary, to give the correct air flow. You can only use a box with ventilation at the sides and/or back to do this, for obvious reasons. A cage is ideal for this purpose as it allows free air flow but the warm air can be contained by throwing a couple of towels over the back half.

Your dog should sit quite happily in the gentle warmth and will dry in there. You may find when you take him out that his rear end is still damp as it was furthest away from the heat and he has been sitting down for most of the time. If this is the case you can give him a quick going-over by hand at the end. Always, of course, finish by brushing him out thoroughly to ensure that there are no matts and tangles left, and to give a nice professional touch. If your dog has been groomed correctly you should be able to go over him to the skin with a comb without effort.

Sun drying

'SUN drying?' I hear you say. 'What, in England? You must be joking'. Well we *do* have the odd days of summer sunshine. Not many, I agree, but on the few occasions when we do, it is well worth having a go at sun drying. I speak, of course, of a really hot day when we can be absolutely certain that there are no clouds in the sky and the sun will be at its peak for a few hours. This is the ideal time to allow a larger dog to dry off. My old Shepherd loves to lie in the sun and I always grab the opportunity to give him a quick bath if the weather is fine.

The most important thing to remember is that the dog must be on a clean surface where he can't roll in the dirt until he is thoroughly dry. This situation can be achieved in several ways; either by securing him with lots of towels on some clean area where he can lie down (remembering that cement gets extremely hot indeed, so beware of that), or you can ideally pop him into his cage, having set it on top of a towel with another towel inside for him to lie on. If you don't set a towel *underneath* the cage, he can roll and dig up the one inside and get to the dirt through the cage floor. *Always allow access to some shade wherever* the dog is situated. If he is in a cage, throw a towel over one side so that he can move into the cooler spot if he wishes. Secure the towel with clothes pegs. NEVER, NEVER, leave a dog restrained in any way if he is in the full sun. He can suffer heatstroke just as quickly as you can. In fact, if the day is really hot with a light breeze he will dry quite happily in the shade.

Always stay close by. Never leave him unattended. Use the situation as

Sun drying

a good excuse to sit out and put your feet up for half-an-hour with a good magazine. This way you can keep glancing over to see if he looks distressed or thirsty. If your dog is obedience trained he will probably sit or lie in the 'down' position by your chair on a large towel with no problems. Beware though, however well trained he is. Keep him on his lead to overcome his desire to run off and roll in the compost heap!

Whatever method of drying you choose, always finish off with a good brush and comb out to remove the final loose hair and the odd matt or tangle which got through the net on the first dry groom out.

Dos and don'ts on drying

Do   Keep on checking the temperature of the dryer to ensure that it isn't too hot. Sometimes the thermostat becomes faulty, so it is essential that you test from time to time.

Do   Offer a drink occasionally, particularly after drying around the facial area, or if the dog appears to be very sensitive to the dryer. If cage drying, place a small drink inside the cage in a spot where it won't get knocked over or, ideally, use one of the clip-on bowls.

Don't   *ever* leave a dog unattended in a cage drying situation. This method is ideal if used correctly as it puts no strain on either the dog or the owner. Most dogs enjoy the gentle warmth so much that they settle down and in next to no time they doze off. This is no excuse to go out to do some gardening or to pop out to the corner shop. It is only common sense to assume that something *could* go wrong (the dryer might overheat for example). So, just have a nice cup of coffee and relax for half an hour in a spot where your dog can see you. Your presence will reassure him that all is well and you can check on him from time to time.

Don't   *ever* apply heat to a dog in any form, either by hand or in a cage-dry situation, if he is wearing either a choke or leather collar, or even a nylon or fabric one if there is any metal evident, such as fasteners, slip rings or identity discs. Why? Because metal conducts heat and BURNS! If you don't believe me, blow a choke chain for a few minutes with a dryer then try to pick it up! When a dog is being dried in a cage he can sit well away from the front bars, but he can't take his own collar off.

This rule is really more important when a dog is being dried by hand, as the heat is directed straight at the animal's body, but it is wise to remove metal-bearing collars in ALL circumstances. If you need something to hold onto during the drying process, use some form of material collar, made perhaps from an old scarf, or even a bit of soft rope. Always remove anything from around the neck as soon as you have finished, to avoid any accidents.

Do   Take your dog outside and make certain that he is fully relieved before he has his bath, and wait at least four hours after his meal. Ideally don't feed until the evening, to ensure his comfort throughout.

Don't   Let him run loose *anywhere* until the following day. If he goes out into the garden after his bath, keep him on his lead, or sure as you're born he will roll and you bet your life he will still be just damp enough to get filthy again. Great sport! I shall always remember one of my own dogs turning green before my very eyes as he rolled in the grass cuttings. What a sight!

Taking stock

Those people who rely on animals for a livelihood, such as farmers, horse trainers, dog breeders and the like, check their stock regularly because vets' bills eat into profits. Pet owners, on the other hand, often fail to detect problems until they have developed to the point where they are painfully visible – to the cost of both the pet and the pocket.

Take a tip from the pros. 'Check your stock' every week of its life. I make it a routine to go over everyone as I groom, checking ears, eyes, teeth and coat. Look out for dry, flaky skin and parasites as you part the hair, and for any small cuts and scratches. These can usually be treated with proprietary pet wound dressings from your first-aid box. You can save a fortune in vet's bills by being sensible and keeping your eyes open.

If you own a dog with shaggy, hairy feet, check between his pads for small foreign objects; bits of twig, tiny stones and hair balls, all of which are often undetectable unless you actually pick up the dog's feet and really root around and feel for them. If they go unnoticed for several days, your dog may well develop sore paws and even a limp, which could result in a hefty vet's bill. It is always a good idea to have the thick hair between the pads taken out by a groomer. This will not spoil the appearance of the dog in any way – I am referring to the thick hair on the actual soles of his feet, between his pads. A good groomer can remove this with either clippers or scissors in a matter of minutes and should charge little for the service. If your dog is very well behaved and steady you may feel that you might like to have a go yourself. If you do, use only sharp but blunt-nosed scissors and ask for the help of a second person to reassure the dog and hold him steady. A dog with 'clean' feet is far less likely to pick up bits of dross when out walking and a big plus is that the feet are easier to wipe dry before coming indoors!

Fleas

It is possible to purchase a puppy from a 'reputable' dealer, only to find that he is infested with fleas. Check him over thoroughly for any indication of parasites. Part the fur in regular rows and look for small black flecks indicating flea dirt or, indeed, the parasites themselves. There are many proprietary brands of insecticidal shampoos and powders on the market and most of them are good, but ideally go to your vet and get a prescribed dip with which to wash the puppy completely, then allow it to dry on him.

Check constantly for parasites throughout hs entire life, as infestation can cause discomfort and misery, particularly from red and broken skin caused by scratching. It is possible for an area to become badly infected by being scratched constantly, bearing in mind that a dog's claws come into contact with the dirt roads and are far from sterile. Again, it is a matter of basic common sense. Remember, fleas can infest your home just as quickly as they can infest your dog – so watch it!

There is no stigma attached to parasite infestation. It can happen in the most immaculate households. Dogs and cats can pick up fleas by just going through the fence into the nextdoor neighbour's garden.

Take particular care in the summer months when the 'little visitors' are at their most active. There is an excellent sheep dip available from vets which, if diluted to the correct proportions for dogs, works wonders, but *do* beware of eyes – it is a great irritant. I often make up a large bucket at full strength and dunk all my dogs' towels and bedding blankets after washing and then just allow them to drip dry on the line. I also use the

To battle! Take arms in the constant fight against parasites (both inside and out). There are many excellent preparations on the market and most can be bought at your local pet store. Your vet will also be very happy to supply your needs. Always follow the instructions to the letter and be extra careful with any insecticidal shampoo and powder around the eyes. Non-stretch flea collars are not good on puppies (see chapter 3) but should be fine on adult dogs who are in constant touch with their owners

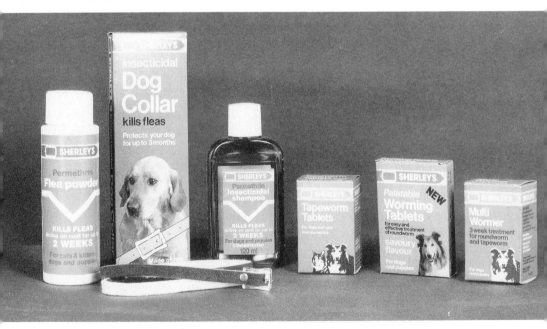

full strength solution in a spray to go over the kennels once a week during the summer months when fleas are at their most active, soaking cracks in the floorboards or any nooks or crannies, not forgetting the underside of the roof. It is amazing just where the little buggers, oops! pardon me, '*bugs*' will get!

Always remember to remove water and feeding bowls before spraying any toxic solution just in case they become polluted; again, common sense. If you have a sleeping box or kennel outside, remember that straw bedding can be a haven for fleas, mainly because one is never quite sure of the straw's origins. If, for example, it is from a farm with free-range poultry it will probably be alive, so beware. It is better to give your dog an old blanket which can be washed out from time to time, than run the risk of parasites.

10

Leisure hours

After the training and grooming comes the happy task of deciding what you and your able canine companion will be doing in your leisure time, and for fun. Here are a few suggestions on hobbies and treats for you and your pet.

R and R

Stands for 'Rest and Recreation' or 'Rack and Ruin'. Which shall it be? A bored dog will look for his own amusement and the latter definitely may well fit the bill. The secret of a happy pet is to give him something to think about. Keep his mind and body active and he won't get into any mischief. A few minutes (ideally several times a day) encouraging your dog to *do* something will ensure that he stays interested and interesting.

Ball or stick play is an ideal way to keep him amused. Most puppies (and dogs) are happy to curl up and rest for several hours after a good play session, just like children, and it's really in both your interests to spare him some time from your busy day.

A play 'fetch' and a controlled 'fetch' are two vastly different things. One is following the stimulus of a moving object for sport and the other is learning an 'unnatural' behaviour i.e. going to an object of any texture or composition which is suitable, picking it up from any position or height within the dog's capabilities, and either holding it, fetching and presenting, or even taking it on to another location and placing it down again. This is 'high school' training and we won't be tackling such advanced manoeuvres at the moment. Let it suffice to encourage our friend to enjoy retrieving for the sheer fun of it. Great sport and exercise, especially if time is limited during the day. A dog can get a great deal of vigorous exercise out of only fifteen or twenty minutes' ball or stick play. If you work part time and you can only pop home for a short spell in the lunch hour, then ball play is absolutely ideal for your dog as it will render him tired and happy to settle when you leave again.

Most puppies can be encouraged to chase a ball and if you are fortunate enough to own one of the 'natural retrievers' you are almost home and dry from the start. The trick is not to throw too far too soon. If you do, your dog may follow the ball with glee, but because you are too far away to encourage him to pick it up, he may well lose interest as it stops moving.

Start by playing around in the house first. Try sitting on the floor in the evening as you watch television and bounce a ball around. As your dog shows interest, just roll it a few feet and if he picks it up take it from him and praise. (You may even give him a little cookie.) If he seems to enjoy the game, try again. It won't take him long to grasp the idea that fetching a ball can be fun. Once he is bringing it back to you from across the carpet you can try in the back garden. Build up distance a bit at a time until in a few short weeks your pet should be bounding across the lawn and fetching his ball back each time.

When training any behaviour a great deal depends upon your attitude! If you want to build up enthusiasm then you must *show* enthusiasm! It's that simple. Dogs cotton on to attitudes very quickly, they are very aware of good and bad vibrations. Each time you throw the ball, jazz him up a bit, get him excited at the prospect and then off you go!

Once the idea of returning the ball to you is imprinted in his computer, try a different object. I have always found a roll of newspaper bound with scotch tape to be ideal, as one may make a stick of any size and thickness, depending upon your dog's type, and it is easily replaced when worn out. Rolled newspaper is kind to the dog's mouth and if he dives on to it, he won't cut himself on any rough edges. If you use a stick, always check it over first for sharp twigs and points. When an enthusiastic dog pounces on to a stick he has no thought for danger. Likewise, make absolutely certain that any ball used is not small enough to get stuck in your dog's throat. Many dogs jump and snap at a bouncing ball and if it is too small and shiny it can very easily get lodged in the back of the mouth. I find a rubber ring an excellent fetch toy; smooth all round and easy to pick up. But it's still a good idea to use a nice bouncy ball in the first place to build up enthusiasm for the game.

You may well get to the point where your dog will fetch objects around the house like the morning paper or slippers. If you use a word each time he actually picks up the object, he will soon associate the command with the action. 'Fido fetch it, go on, good dog, fetch it.' This will make the task of teaching advanced retrieving so much easier if you decide to go on at a later date.

'Tug of war' is great sport and all my dogs love it. I knot together my son's old socks and use those. We have a great time testing each other's strength. My young Jack Russell loves the game so much he will jump up and hang on to the socks with glee, convincing himself that by giving them a good shake, he is master of the situation. If I let go he will run off into a corner with his prey and 'kill' it. I'm often coming across 'dead' socks hidden behind the sofa.

An active dog is a happy dog so try to find a little time each day to have a game with your pet. You will both enjoy it (dead socks and all)!

Watch the birdie

Now your pet is nicely behaved, why not try your hand at some animal photography? I love a good challenge and it's certainly that! Great fun and useful too. It's quite possible to produce some super shots with the simplest of cameras and these pictures may be used in many ways, from making your own greeting cards and calendars to posters and coasters etc. Super gifts for all occasions.

Keep your subjects simple. Over-dressed shots are 'noisy' and distracting to the eye. Think up a few situations which could be used for any purpose. The most important thing to remember is, if shooting indoors, one must have a perfectly plain background. Domestic situations really don't make good 'professional' shots (with the possible exception of a fireside picture).

If you have nice plain emulsioned walls – perfect! Take account of the colour of your carpet in relation to your pet and if you have a brown dog don't ask him to sit on a brown floor. His top half will stand out nicely against the plain wall but at the lower end the two browns will merge. Find a light-coloured towel or sheet and lay it down against the wall and sit your subject on that. Never lay your cloth directly on top of the carpet if you want a professional shot. Place a sheet of plywood or something firm underneath and secure the sides to ensure the fabric stays taut. If you don't do this your dog's feet will sink into the soft surface, making creases and shadowy dents.

Many smaller dogs will stay still longer if up high (some larger ones too). If you have a rock-steady table strong enough to hold your pet, push that up against the wall and cover it with a cloth of an appropriate colour. Plain pastel shades work well for most, but of course never put a white dog onto a white sheet – you will hardly see him in the shot. Red and green are both fine for Christmas pictures and one can produce some super festive cards for very little effort and expense.

A few simple props are all that will be required. A bit of tinsel, a pretty

Watch the birdie!

'Boring'
Fancy asking a chap to leave a nice smelly bone and pose for a soppy photo. Can't wait to get back into the garden again. Don't reckon much to this modelling lark myself!

Everything is wrong with this photo of Danny. The little dog is plainly disinterested in the whole procedure. He is obediently 'staying' in the 'down' position but his mind is on other things. He appears to have a paw missing as he tucks it under him and his ears are down. His eyes are wasted as they are not looking at anything in particular

pot plant with a ribbon/bow, perhaps primroses or violets, a little vase of anemones (with no water in case of spillage) can work wonders when placed next to a beautiful dog of small to medium size. Larger dogs look better with 'stronger' props such as pipe and slippers or maybe a log or lump of bark with a few pine cones. Have fun experimenting.

Place your dog against the background in your required position. The 'down' is really the best to start with as it is a nice steady situation which will prevent any 'wobbles'. Ask your pet to 'stay' and reassure him. If you have help from a second person all to the good. Stroke your pet and hold

'Rabbits!! Who said rabbits?'
 Hard to believe but true. Same dog, same camera setting. Photos taken five minutes apart. The addition of a few simple props makes for a much more professional shot. Note that both front paws are now visible. The wonderful animated expression is achieved by the use of a few interesting sounds and words. Result, magic!

on to him whilst your helper fires the flash a couple of times before you start. Your dog will soon learn that it won't hurt him and will sit still. If you have to give him a treat as a reward, remember to use clean food which won't mark the 'set up' if he drops it. Dry biscuits are usually the best as one can brush the crumbs away. Try to work without food if possible.

Now we have our subject in position, place your prop next to him. Step back behind the camera and repeat 'staaay' in a nice steady tone. Then (here's a trick of the trade!) *stop talking to him* and just show him the hand signal. Keep completely silent for a moment, try to hold his attention, and have your finger on the trigger ready to shoot. This really isn't easy on one's own. It's better as a two-man job. Let someone else fire the camera or use a remote 'trigger' if you are doing it yourself. Your dog should be sitting or lying still and taking notice of your silent signal.

Now take a squeaky toy or something which may spark off an animated expression without getting the dog excited enough to break. The squeak usually works well. Just one squeak and the head should flick over to one side. Squeak and shoot simultaneously and the results can be magic. The trick is to make the sound a complete surprise. The resulting picture will be far more interesting than a straightforward pose! If the dog becomes familiar with the squeak it won't work, so don't waste it in practice. Just get ready and *shoot*! Have confidence. If you 'wear out' one noise, move on to another. Say, a mouth organ or a whistle. Anything really which will animate the expression without disturbing the subject.

It's a challenge, but so rewarding when it works. Do have a go. Once you get bitten by the bug, you will constantly be trying for better pictures. Outdoor shots are always very natural and the same method can be used there. A lovely Setter sitting in a corn field may be magically brought to life with a sudden squeak or whistle. You just have to practise at being 'quick on the draw'. When you get the perfect shot it makes the whole thing well worth the effort.

I consider myself very fortunate to work regularly with one of the world's leading animal photographers, Arthur Sidey. We have, over the years, built up a super working relationship whereby we almost know what each other is thinking. Arthur loves a challenge and if I can set the picture up, he can take it. We have never been beaten yet and our photos are syndicated all round the world. Pippin must, without doubt, be one of the.most photographed dogs in the 'biz'; a true international model!

Your dog can do just as well for you with time and practice. I recommend that you have a go. Surprise yourself – you will be delighted at the results of your efforts. A few simple rules: never use a direct flash when photographing animals. If you do you will get 'white eyes' and the picture will be spoiled. If you can get someone to hold the flash on a lead, just offset from the subject, all to the good, or try to set up a picture with strong natural lighting where a flash isn't necessary. If you pride yourself on being a bit of a David Bailey and you have a few lights, great! Even better.

Set your subject in place and focus. Then remove the dog and mark the spot exactly with tape, laying the strips at the angle the dog will be lying. Replace the dog with a stuffed toy of similar size and colour and use that to set up your lighting. If you don't use a stand-in, by the time you are set

One of Pippin's best-known photographs (Daily Mirror)

All creatures great and small! (Daily Mirror)

to shoot, your dog will have lost interest and look fed up and bored. Plus, of course, we do not wish to put any stress on him. He will happily sit for a few minutes at a time but it's unfair to ask him to stay in one spot for too long.

When you are set, replace your dog and re-check your focus. Place your 'prop' in position and you are ready to shoot. If you are actually taking the photo yourself, get someone else to attract the dog's attention, or *vice versa*. If you are shooting alone, the only way is to 'set' your camera and use a remote trigger and look him in the eyes. Get his attention in the requested direction and shoot.

The eyes have it

Eyes are vital. The whole character of the animal is reflected in the eyes. I personally love to see a photo where the subject is looking straight at me; there is an instant 'bond'. Slightly offset eyes are O.K. too if the subject is looking at something interesting. (See photo of my German Shepherd, Max, with the ducklings.) No eyes at all make for a very ordinary picture. (See the 'before' and 'after' shots of Danny on pages 110 and 111).

So there we are. Go on! Have a go! You may surprise yourself and discover that you have talent. It's a super hobby. I do recommend evening classes for beginners. They are readily available at most local technical colleges. One last comment on the subject. There is no point in taking a good set-up photograph of a dog if the animal isn't properly groomed (happy family snaps excepted of course). Don't spoil a good shot by having it processed and discovering 'sleep' in the corners of the eyes or saliva matts around the mouth. No professional animal should go into a studio situation without as much preparation as any top model girl. Give your dog a thorough grooming before you consider using an expensive film.

It's that little extra time and effort which will make all the difference. Good luck!

Christmas 'crackers'

Gifts for pets. Good heavens! Whatever next? Big business in the USA and starting to become popular over here. But why pay out large sums of money on presents for your dog when you can make some super things very cheaply? I always put a small present under the tree for each of my animals – including my daughter's Cockatiel! Daft I suppose, but I enjoy doing it and I think that the pets like it too. Pippin and several of the other

Pippin's cot full of fairly uniform 'Christmas Crackers' (Daily Mirror) who grew in no time at all into a trunk load of 'Dolly Mixtures'. By the way, if you are counting noses, when the photograph opposite was taken, two little rascals had already gone on to their new homes! (Bracknell News)

dogs are capable of opening their own parcels and we help the rest to open theirs. Everyone gets a little something on Christmas morning.

Home-made dog biscuits are ideal as they will store in an airtight tin or even freeze and they can be packaged as if they were straight from Fortnums - great if you want to impress your friends. They sometimes look so tempting that one is inclined to have just the odd nibble (to ensure freshness, you understand)! Then there is the non-spill water drinker. This is easily made from a large margarine or ice-cream carton and is absolutely *invaluable* when travelling as one can leave a drink with a dog without any possibility of spillage in the back of the car (real Blue Peter stuff this)!

Or sew your own dog jacket. Very simple to do, even if you are (like me) not much of a seamstress. Go into a pet shop and take a sneaky look at the dog coats on show. They are so straightforward that one really doesn't even need a pattern. Just a basic 'saddle' shape in a size to fit your pet, with snap or velcro fastenings. Always allow free access to the 'waterworks' department. Make absolutely sure that none of the flaps or straps restrict the call of nature, and off you go! One may use any material of suitable weight to keep out the cold and possibly cover with plastic to render it waterproof.

A simply made non-spill drinker has many uses. Ideal for travelling if only filled to the three-quarter level (maximum), it shouldn't slop around in the car. Also ideal for dogs with long ears which tend to droop into an ordinary bowl

Care must be taken to ensure that the opening is large enough for a dog to drink with ease and without any possibility of getting his head stuck. This type of drinker is great for dogs with long muzzles

The pictures are self-explanatory: just take any large plastic carton container with a nice fitting lid (catering size ice-cream or margarine cartons are ideal). Take off the lid and draw and cut around an object of a suitable size, making a nice smooth hole. (File away any rough edges of course.) Fill with water, replace the lid and hey presto! Your pet will lap it up (Daily Mirror)

Home-made dog biscuits. Don't I deserve one?

Noodles looking very swish and superior in her jumper made from a sleeve out of an old 'sloppy Joe' sweater

Noodles is wearing the very latest in the sleeve of an old sweater (the top of an old leg warmer or sleeve of a large cardigan will do just as well). Note the buttonhole finish and neatly turned edges! Straight out of Vogue, I do declare!

This basic idea can be adapted in various sizes for different breeds from any odd items of clothing, even perhaps using a large sock to make a sweater for a tiny chihuahua. Take the top of the sock, measure from the dog's waist to the elbow and cut two small holes for the front legs. Keep the openings reasonably large so the edges don't chafe the top of the little dog's legs and then to prevent fraying, finish off in a nice contrasting coloured wool. Do the bottom cut edge to match and there you are. Very posh!

Actually, there is a serious side to this. One may feel a bit of a twerp walking the streets with a dressed-up pooch (although personally I don't think it matters a jot what other folks think). But if you own an old or

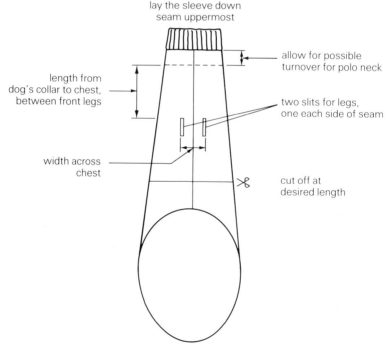

length from dog's collar to chest, between front legs

lay the sleeve down seam uppermost

allow for possible turnover for polo neck

two slits for legs, one each side of seam

width across chest

cut off at desired length

finish off all cut edges with buttonhole stitching or something similar. Try to catch all loose threads to prevent fraying, but don't pull too tight – allow for stretching over the back and legs. If binding is used, the coat should be stretched and fitted first to ensure there is enough 'give' to prevent chafing

Making a coat from the sleeve of an old sweater

invalid pet then this cover-all can be a godsend. If a dog is out for a *brisk* walk getting the old heart pumping and the circulation working well, then the coat God gave him is more than adequate, but if your pet is a bit infirm and susceptible to the cold the change in temperature first thing in the morning can be quite traumatic for him. If you send him out into the garden for his potter and pee straight from the central heating into the bitter cold, this little body warmer can be invaluable. His dignity will be preserved as no-one will see him in the privacy of his own 'patch' and he will thank you for it. Many older dogs visibly shiver if their hair is wearing a bit thin and they are glad of a bit of help from their friends.

Dog blankets are welcome gifts. Made from any old bits of washable material, edged perhaps with nice coloured binding and maybe embroidered with the pet's name. In order to keep on top of the flea population it is essential to change and wash bedding regularly, so one cannot have too many blankets! Crochet ones are lovely. And very luxurious, made from odd balls of wool, or even from the yarn of unpicked sweaters. I have to admit I'm not much good at knitting, but even I can manage a nifty treble stitch with my crochet hook.

For the dog who has everything in the way of garments and blankets, how about a tasty treat for special occasions? Here are a few gastronomic delights for you to try out on your days off.

Bowser's Beefy Biscuits

Ingredients:

    1 cup rolled oatmeal   (Porridge Oats)
    1 cup wholemeal flour
    1 large egg
    1 dessertspoon Bovril
    A little milk to mix

Method

Mix together the flour, oatmeal, egg and Bovril and work in well with a wooden spoon. Add just enough milk to form a nice stiff, but workable, dough.

Turn onto a floured board and roll out to about the thickness of two one pound coins on top of each other ($\frac{1}{2}$ cm).

Cut into interesting shapes and bake on a lightly greased tray at 175°C (330°F) for 15 minutes. Allow to completely cool and store in an airtight container or freeze.

Cheesy Chewies

Ingredients:

    1 cup rolled oatmeal
    1 cup wholemeal flour
    1 large egg
    ½ cup grated 'mouse trap' cheese
    1 teaspoon grated Parmesan (for aroma and flavour)
    Milk to mix

Method

Make as for Beefy Biscuits, substituting the cheeses for Bovril. These biscuits smell lovely when baking. The Parmesan certainly 'spikes' them up. All my dogs and some of the cats like them. Do remember to watch the old waistline though! These are special treats only (or take the calories into account at meal times)!

While on the subject of cooking – what do you do with the drippings from your grill pan? I keep a tin of biscuit meal in the kitchen and pour the fat over this and mix it well in. After a day or two, when I have added enough fat to saturate the meal, I mix it into the large bin of biscuit which I use at feeding times. Animal fat is a natural food for dogs, but of course like anything else it can be over-done, so for this reason I always stir the fatty meal into some dry meal before serving. My dogs eat it with relish!

'Dem bones'

Of course, no-one in their right minds would serve chicken on the bone to a dog. The consequences could be disastrous, but there is no need to waste any bones left over after a meal.

I have an old iron pan, my 'dog stock pot', which is used for nothing else. *All* bones (any type of meat) left over from either the plates or the joints are put into the pan, brought to the boil and then simmered for an hour or so. The liquid is then strained into a large basin and allowed to completely cool. This forms a marvellous jelly stock which may be mixed with the food, either cold or warmed up again in small quantities and poured over the pet's meal. If your dog is overweight or susceptible to too much fat, skim it off first. Stock is wonderful for animals with finicky appetites and, of course, invalids can be tempted to eat with the addition of a little cold chicken jelly. When everything else fails, powdered vitamins and medications can easily be disguised in stock, with a flavour strong enough to fool even the most discerning of appetites.

Cooked marrow bones are excellent for keeping a dog's teeth in pristine condition, so if you are fortunate enough to have a butcher who will save a few for you, and will saw them into reasonable sizes, great! Boil them up first in the stock pot to take advantage of the jelly which they will produce and then after they have cooled down, allow your pet to enjoy one as a treat. Outside of course, as they do make nasty greasy marks on the floor. Most dogs will bury a bone and then dig it up again when it has got nice and smelly. So try, if you can, to retrieve your pet's treasure before he gets the chance to play Long John Silver with it. Much more pleasant! When he gets round to the second sitting it will have got rather 'high', to say the least! Not very desirable, however tasty!

Something for everybody – after all, a good dog deserves a little luxury now and then. Have fun!

11

The end of the line

My old Shepherd Smokey fell asleep last summer. He lay down in the garden and didn't wake. I shed many tears but was grateful for the manner in which he drifted away, in a quiet, dignified sleep. No pain, no previous telltale warnings of his passing despite his twelve years of age.

He had lived with us throughout his entire life – he was born here, and together with his brother Max, he had travelled halfway round the world and back, spending six and a half years in America and returning through quarantine with Max and little Pippin for company.

If your pet, like Smokey, is lucky enough to die of old age, you will be very fortunate. Sadly, it doesn't always work that way.

Many pedigree dogs develop hereditary defects early in life and have their days on this earth cut short. Others are the victims of unfortunate circumstances, accidents or disease. Their owners may have to make the decision between life and death. I have been faced with this decision and I can tell you that it is not easy.

If your vet feels that your pet's life will no longer be worth living you will be paying him the ultimate tribute by relieving his suffering. If we search our souls and are scrupulously honest with ourselves, we know deep down that it is the thought of parting which makes us hesitate. Let us not be selfish under these circumstances and try to be brave. To relieve pain and suffering *must* be a kindness. Far better to remember happier times than to watch a friend waste away.

Coping with bereavement is never easy, and to many people losing a beloved pet is as tragic as losing a member of the family. The grief lies deep and is hard to bear. Friends and family try to offer help and consolation but in the end, it is up to us to come to terms with the situation. If our canine friend dies of old age, in a peaceful and painless manner, we must be thankful for that and try to remember the good days and the warm and loving relationship that we had built up over the years.

No other dog can ever take the place of a lost companion. We must accept each newcomer on his own merit. It would be unfair to compete with past excellence just as it is unfair to compare different members of the family. Each puppy born brings its own love and so it will be with your next canine pal. He *will* be different and sometimes exasperating because he may not be as quick to learn a certain behaviour as was his predecessor. (But then again he may be streets ahead in other ways.) One thing is for sure, if you give him the chance, he will be *just* as willing to devote his life to you. His presence will help to fill the void and the sooner you invite him to share your life the sooner you'll begin to get over your loss.

Your old dog will never be forgotten; of course not. But the newcomer will give you a fresh start, an opportunity to build another lasting, loving relationship and when you feel down in the dumps, his cold wet nose and soft brown eyes will be a comfort. You will have him there just as you had your old friend. For the pleasure of his company.